Arbor Legis

The Tree of Law

ESHAAN VASUDEV, CLAIRE TIAN, ANDREW MILLS,
RONALD D. ROESSLER, MD

ILLUSTRATED BY AIDA EL-HAJJAR & MIA LUCKE

Milwaukee, Wisconsin

TABLE OF CONTENTS

PREFACE

In an era of complex legal systems and global connections, understanding the Latin origins of legal terms and phrases builds a crucial foundation for students, professionals, and engaged citizens.

For students, this knowledge not only broadens their vocabularies but also enhances their analytical and communication skills, which are essential for future academic and professional success. Additionally, learning legal terminology provides a first step to understanding the principles, rights, and responsibilities that shape our societies.

This book is a sequel to *Arbor Medicinae* and aims to be a valuable starting resource for anyone who wants to learn more about the roots at the base of our ever-growing "tree of law," including aspiring lawyers, students, advocates, classical scholars, and curious people in general. By exploring Latin legal terms and phrases, we also connect to the world of ancient Rome and to legal traditions from around the globe that continue to draw on its lasting influence.

COMMON PREPOSITIONS

ad - towards
a/ab - from
contra - against
cum - with, together
de - from/away from, about
dis - apart
e/ex/extra - out, outside
in - on, into
inter - amongst, between
ne - not
non - not
ob - over, to
per - through
post - after
prae/pre - before
pro - for, on behalf of
re - back, undo, again
se - apart
sine - without
sub - under, beneath, up from under
super - above

Note that if there are any prepositions with irregular/special meanings, those will be defined in the term.

GENERAL LEGAL TERMINOLOGY

Section II

Section III

Section IV

Section V

This chapter introduces the core vocabulary that is used across law. You will encounter many of these terms or phrases in all sorts of places, whether it be in the news or in everyday discussions.

Knowing these terms and phrases will broaden your knowledge of law and legal reasoning, and sharpen your understanding of how our laws apply.

Examples of General Legal Terminology:

- Ad hoc
- Bona fide
- Per se
- Verdict

Ab initio

ab + initium, initii - beginning

Literally means "from the beginning." Used when to indicate something from the outset; often used as part of the phrase "void ab initio"

Ad hoc

ad + hoc - this

Literally means "for this". Created or done for a specific purpose or case, such as an ad hoc committee, and not meant to be permanent.

Ad hoc

The UN Security Council created temporary ad hoc criminal tribunals specifically for the former Yugoslavia (1993) and Rwanda (1994) conflicts

Ad infinitum

ad + infinitus - endless, infinity

Literally means "to infinity". Describes something that could continue without end.

Ad nauseam

ad + nausea, nauseae - seasickness

Literally means "to a sickening (degree)". Used when a point or legal argument is repeated to an excessive and tiresome extent.

OTHER RELATED TERMS

initial (*initium*)
confine (*infinitum*)
finite (*infinitum*)
noise (*nausea*)

A fortiori

a + fortis, forte - strong

Literally means "from the stronger". An inference that if a stronger argument, rule, or penalty is accepted, the weaker version must also hold.

Animus

animus, animi - mind

Literally means "motive". Refers to a person's intent or mental state when acting.

A priori

a + prior - before

Literally means "from the previous". Reasoning from general principles rather than specific evidence.

Bona fide

bonus - good + fides, fidei - faith

Literally means "in good faith". Acting with honest intent (i.e. A bona fide purchaser who buys a house without notice of an earlier unrecorded claim may keep clear title).

Animus

In *Romer v. Evans* (1996), the U.S. Supreme Court struck down Colorado's Amendment 2, holding that a law motivated by bare animus toward a group violates the Equal Protection Clause.

OTHER RELATED TERMS

comfort (*fortis*)
animation (*animus*)
prioritize (*prior*)
confidence (*fides*)

De facto

de + factum, facti - fact, deed

Literally means "from the fact", better known as "in fact". A condition existing in practice even if not formally recognized by law.

De jure

de - concerning + ius, iuris - law, right

Literally means "by right". A condition that is legally recognized, whether or not it exists in practice.

De minimis (non curat lex)

de + minimus - smallest + non + curare - to care + lex, legis - law

Literally means "the law does not care of minimal things". Courts often disregard insignificant matters.

Injunction

iniungere - to join together

A court order requiring a party to do (mandatory) or refrain from doing (prohibitory) a specific act.

Injunction
The Nixon administration sought an injunction to block the Pentagon Papers, which was denied by the U.S. Supreme Court in *New York Times Co. v. United States* (1971).

OTHER RELATED TERMS

factor (*factum*)
injury (*ius*)
minimize (*minimus*)
adjust (*iungere*)

Inter alia

inter + alius - other

Literally means "among other things". Indicates the point mentioned is one of several (e.g. A judge says, "The court found, inter alia, that the contract was breached.").

Ipso facto

ipse - itself + factum, facti - fact, deed

Literally means "by the fact itself". Something follows directly from a stated fact.

Ipso jure

ipse - itself + ius, iuris - law, right

Literally means "by the law itself." A result that follows automatically by operation of law.

Jurisdiction

ius, iuris - law, right + dicere - to speak

A court's authority to hear a case and render a binding judgement.

Jurisdiction
In ***Marbury v. Madison*** (1803), the U.S. Supreme Court held it lacked jurisdiction to issue a writ of mandamus and, as a result, established judicial review.

OTHER RELATED TERMS

alias (*alius*)
affect (*factum*)
conjure (*ius*)
dictionary (*dicere*)

Jurisprudence

ius, iuris - law, justice + prudentia, prudentiae - wisdom

The study of law in a philosophical or theoretical sense; also used for the body of case law in a legal system.

Liability

ligare - to bind, tie

Legal responsibility for one's actions or omissions, such as the obligation to remedy harm.

Litigation

lis, litis - lawsuit, quarrel + agere - to drive forward

Resolving disputes through the court system.

Mutatis mutandis

mutare - to change

Literally means "with the necessary changes having been made". Demonstrates that a statement or rule can be applied to a new context with appropriate adjustments.

Liability

In ***Donoghue v Stevenson*** (1932), the House of Lords (UK) held that manufacturers owe consumers a duty of care even without a contract ("neighbour principle").

OTHER RELATED TERMS

prudent (*prudens*)
obligation (*ligare*)
agitate (*agere*)
mutate (*mutare*)

Per se

per + se - itself

Literally means "by itself". Indicates something is inherently so.

Prima facie

primus - first + facies, faciei - face, appearance

Literally means "at first appearance". Evidence sufficient to establish a fact unless rebutted.

Pro bono (publico)

pro + bonus, boni - good + publicus - public

Literally means "for the public good". Legal services provided without charge to those unable to pay.

Pro forma

pro + forma, formae - form, shape

Literally means "for the sake of form". Done to satisfy procedure or formality rather than contain substance.

Pro forma

In *NLRB v. Noel Canning* (2014), the U.S. Supreme Court held that the Senate's pro forma sessions count as being in session, limiting recess appointments.

OTHER RELATED TERMS

ampersand (*se*)
facet (*facies*)
beneficial (*bonus*)
conform (*forma*)

Pro rata

pro + reri - to think

Literally means "in proportion". Allocation or calculation based on a defined base (e.g. ownership percentage, time period, or amount owned), not equal shares.

Pro tempore

pro + tempus, temporis - time

Literally means "for the time being". Serving in a role temporarily when the usual officeholder is unavailable.

Pro tempore

In 2023, Patty Murray (WA) became the first woman President pro tempore of the U.S. Senate, a role that presides when the Vice President is absent, and is third in the presidential line of succession.

Quasi

quasi - as if

Literally means "as if". Resembling something but not actually the same, such as having some but not all legal attributes.

Status quo

status, status - position, state + qui - who, which

Literally means "the state in which". The existing state of affairs, often preserved pending resolution of a dispute.

OTHER RELATED TERMS

ration (*reri*)
contemporary (*tempus*)
quasar (*quasi*)
superstition (*status*)

Stet

stare - to stand

Literally means "let it stand". Indicates an indefinite postponement of prosecution.

Stricto sensu

strictus - tight, close + sensus, sensus - sense

Literally means "in the strict sense". Signals a narrow, technical reading of language.

Sui generis

suus - its own + genus, generis - kind, origin

Literally means "of its own kind". Something unique that doesn't fit established categories (e.g. In intellectual property, certain ship hull designs can be granted "sui generis" protection).

Verdict

verus - true + dicere - to speak

A formal decision on issues in a case, usually by a jury. In criminal cases, it determines guilt, while in civil cases, it determines liability and often damages.

Verdict

In *Ramos v. Louisiana* (2020), the U.S. Supreme Court held that guilty verdicts in state criminal trials must be unanimous, overruling *Apodaca v. Oregon* (1972).

OTHER RELATED TERMS

resistant (*stare*)
resentful (*sensus*)
genius (*genus*)
verify (*verus*)

One evening on Olympus, Themis, goddess of law, gathered her daughters in a court hall. Eunomia, meaning "Good Order," stood straight, with a scroll of laws clasped in her hands. Dike, the goddess of Justice, held a golden scale that gleamed even in the shadows.

However, across the marble floor slunk Adikia, the goddess of Injustice. Her smile assumed the form of ignorance, and her hands were stained from deceit. She laughed at her sisters and whispered into their ears, "Why follow laws when deception can profit more?" Wherever she walked, Trust fled from her sight.

Themis calmly spoke, "Law without justice is pointless. Justice without law is to no avail. When these aren't balanced equally on a scale, Injustice enters the court." Eunomia placed her scroll on the ground, and Dike set her scales beside it; together, they drove Adikia away from the court and back into the shadows.

Laws (Eunomia) and justice (Dike) must always coexist in all societies, as all societies have injustice (Adikia).

While no single myth survives of Themis and her daughters with Adikia, ancient poets and painters often depicted them as opposed to each other. Hesiod called Eunomia and Dike Horae, guardians of civilization, while Pausanias in Athens saw a depiction of Dike striking down Adikia.

PRIVATE LAW

PRIVATE LAW CONSISTS OF THE FOLLOWING:

Family Law: Rules governing marriage and divorce, parentage, custody and visitation, support obligations, and the allocation of property within families.

Contract Law: Formation, interpretation, performance, and breach of agreements, including defenses and remedies such as damages and specific performance.

Tort Law: Civil liability for harm, from negligence to intentional torts and strict liability, with attention to duty, causation, damages, and defenses.

Property Law: Rights in land and personal property, including ownership, possession, estates and future interests, transfers, and landlord–tenant relations.

Coroporate Law: Organization and governance of business entities, fiduciary duties, shareholder rights, corporate transactions, and basic securities concepts.

Ab intestato

ab + intestatus - intestate, having made no will

Literally means "from an intestate (died without a will)." The estate is distributed under intestacy statutes.

Actio in personam

actio, actionis - action + in - against + persona, personae - person

Literally means "action against a person". A lawsuit seeking to impose personal liability on a defendant.

Adoption

ad + optare - to choose, wish

The legal process by which an adult becomes the child's legal parent, with all parental rights and duties.

Annulment

ad + nullus, nulli - none, nothing

A judicial degree that a marriage was invalid from the start, as if it never existed.

Ab intestato

The musician Prince died without a will in 2016, so Minnesota intestacy law determined his heirs.

OTHER RELATED TERMS

action (*actio*)
personality (*persona*)
adopt (*optare*)
nullify (*nullus*)

Cohabitation

cum + habitare - to live, dwell

Living together as partners without marriage. Often addressed by cohabitation agreements or domestic-partnership laws to clarify property, expenses, and support.

Custody

custos, custodis - guardian, protector

A guardian's legal authority and physical care of a child.

Domicile

domus, domi - house + colere - to dwell

An individual's fixed, permanent living space, to which they intend to return someday. Requires physical presence and intent; a person may have many residences but only one domicile at a time.

Emancipation

e + manus, manus - hand + capere - to take

A way for a minor to legally detach themselves from their guardian.

Cohabitation

In *Marvin v. Marvin* (1976), the court held that nonmartial partners who cohabited may enforce express or implied agreements about property or support (palimony).

OTHER RELATED TERMS

habitat (*habitare*)
custodian (*custos*)
domestic (*domus*)
manifest (*manus*)

In loco parentis

in + locus, loci - place + parens, parentis - parent

Literally means "in the place of a parent". The role of a person or institution acting with limited parental duties/powers.

Ne exeat

ne + exire - to go

Literally means "let him not leave". A court order restraining a person from leaving a jurisdiction or area (e.g. The United States' phrase is "ne exeat republica," meaning "let him not leave the republic").

Nuptial

nubere - to marry

Relating to marriage.

Parens patriae

parens, parentis - parent + patria, patriae - fatherland, country

Literally means "parent of the country". A state or court's parental or protective responsibilities to its citizens.

Ne exeat

In *Abbott v. Abbott* (2010), the U.S. Supreme Court held that a ne exeat order gives a "right of custody", allowing the child's return if taken abroad.

OTHER RELATED TERMS

couch (*locus*)
exit (*exire*)
connubile (*nubere*)
patronage (*patria*)

Paternity

pater, patris - father

Legal fatherhood; establishing or proving a man's status as a child's father. May be established by the marital presumption, a voluntary acknowledgement, or a court order after genetic testing, triggering rights and duties such as custody, visitation, support, and inheritance.

Residence

re + sedere - to sit

The place where an individual resides at a specific moment, which may be temporary.

Surrogacy

sub + rogare - to ask, propose

When a woman carries a pregnancy for intended parents who will raise the child when it is born.

Visitation

videre - to see

Court-ordered parenting time for a noncustodial parent. Orders may specify schedules, exchanges, and, where needed, supervised visitation, and can be modified upon a material change in circumstances.

Visitation

In *Troxel v. Granville* (2000), the U.S. Supreme Court held that broad third-party visitation laws violate a fit parent's due process right to direct a child's upbringing and that courts must give special weight to the parent's decisions.

OTHER RELATED TERMS

perpetrate (*pater*)
president (*sedere*)
interrogate (*rogare*)
visible (*videre*)

FAMILY LAW

In the crowded basilicas of Rome, Cicero knew that words alone rarely won a case. A lawyer also needed to be fluent in the art of stagecraft. While planning a case, he called the plaintiff's children into the forum, making them pale and dressed plainly to induce pity in the iudices (judges). Even the most impartial iudex could be moved by a weeping widow in mourning attire. On the other hand, a witness in a toga praetexta or trabea demonstrated a certain level of respectability, authority, and responsibility. The court has now permanently become a theater where actors make their cases. Even today, a family seated behind opposing counsel's table can silently argue the case just as strongly as the lawyer's closing statement.

Acquisition

ad + quaerere - to seek, obtain

The purchase of control or assets of one company by another. May be a stock purchase or an asset purchase.

Affiliate

affiliare - to adopt a son

A company related by common control (i.e. power to direct management or policies), whether or not majority ownership exists. Includes, parents, subsidiaries, and sister companies.

Capital

caput, capitis - head

Financial resources of a business; includes equity and debt. Share capital refers to owners' paid-in equity, not market capitalization.

Consolidation

cum + solidare - to make solid

The combination of companies into a new entity, with the constituents ceasing to exist. All assets, liabilities, and contracts transfer to the new entity at the effective time.

Acquisition

Microsoft completed its acquisition of Activision Blizzard in 2023 after regulatory review for $75.4 billion, making it the largest deal in video-game history.

OTHER RELATED TERMS

inquire (*quaerere*)
filial (*affiliare*)
captain (*caput*)
soldier (*solidare*)

Corporation

corpus, corporis - body

A legal entity separate from its owners. It can own property, enter contracts, sue and be sued, and usually provides limited liability and perpetual existence.

Director

dirigere - to set right

A member of a corporation's board charged with overseeing management and corporate affairs. Directors are elected by shareholders, appoint officers, set policy, and owe fiduciary duties of care and loyalty.

Dividend

dividere - to separate

A distribution of a corporation's profits to shareholders. Dividends are declared by the board and may be paid in cash, stock, or property. However, they aren't guaranteed.

Fiduciary

fidus - faithful

A person who owes duties of loyalty and care to another. Must act in the other's best interest, avoid conflicts of interest, and exercise prudence.

Fiduciary

In *Guth v. Loft* (1939), the court held that usurping a corporate opportunity (Guth taking Pepsi-Cola for himself) breaches the fiduciary duty of loyalty.

OTHER RELATED TERMS

corset (*corpus*)
regal (*dirigere*)
divisible (*dividere*)
fiancee (*fidus*)

Governance

gubernare - to direct, rule

The rules and practices by which a company is directed and controlled.

Merger

mergere - to dip in, plunge, overwhelm

The combination of companies where one survives and assumes the other's assets and liabilities.

Noncompete

non + cum + petere - to strive, seek

A contract term that bars an employee or seller from competing, such as working for a rival, soliciting clients, or using confidential information, for a set time and within a defined area.

Option

optare - to choose, wish

A contractual right to buy or sell shares or assets at a set price within a period. (e.g. stock options give the holder the right to purchase shares at a strike price).

Merger

The largest merger in history was AOL and Time Warner, announced January 10, 2000, valued at about $182 billion.

OTHER RELATED TERMS

emergency (*mergere*)
submersible (*mergere*)
appetite (*petere*)
coopt (*optare*)

Partnership

pars, partis - part, piece

An association of two or more persons carrying on a business as co-owners, sharing profits and liabilities.

Prospectus

pro - forward + specere - to look at

Literally means "having looked forward". A disclosure document for prospective investors describing a securities offering.

Proxy

pro + curare - to care for

A contract term that bars an Authority granted to another to vote one's shares; can refer to the person or instrument that carries the authority.

Subsidiary

sub + sedere - to sit

A company controlled by another company. Control usually means having more than 50 percent of voting power or the practical ability to elect the board and direct policies.

Prospectus
The Securities Act of 1933 requires issuers in registered public offerings to provide a prospectus with material information for investors.

OTHER RELATED TERMS

particle (*pars*)
introspection (*specere*)
curious (*curare*)
residue (*sedere*)

CORPORATE LAW

In the Forum of Trajan, merchants once gathered beneath marble porticoes to make agreements that are familiar to a corporate lawyer today. A shipping guild could fund road paving in exchange for tax concessions, while a group of traders could combine their wealth to sponsor a new temple as both an act of piety and of public relationship building. Contracts were made official by being carved into wax tablets, like our legal documents today. The wealth of Rome was burgeoned through trust, reputations, and relationships. A temple to Mercury (patron of commerce) could rise from collective financing just as easily as modern skyscrapers. Even the roads that stretched outward from the city were funded by public contributions, bringing goods such as olive oil, glass, and grain across the empire. What seemed ancient was already changing the way corporate matters work today, where groups of people used law and wealth to build their prestige and further profits.

Caveat emptor

cavere - to beware + emptor, emptoris - buyer

Literally means "let the buyer beware". Places the risk on the purchaser to inspect before purchase.

Consensus ad idem

consensus, consensus - agreement + ad + idem - the same

Literally means "agreement to the same thing". A binding contract requires a meeting of the minds on essential terms.

Consensus ad idem
In *Raffles v. Wichelhaus* (1864), no contract formed because each party meant a different ship called *Peerless*.

Consideration

cum + sidus, sideris - star, constellation

The bargained-for exchange that makes a promise enforceable. Each party must give value; past consideration is generally invalid.

Contra bonos mores

contra + bonus - good + mos, moris - custom, moral

Literally means "against good morals". Agreements contrary to public policy are unenforceable.

OTHER RELATED TERMS

caution (*cavere*)
sensation (*consensus*)
desire (*sidus*)
morale (*mos*)

Contra proferentem

contra + proferre - to bring forward

Literally means "against the offerer". Ambiguous terms are construed against the party who drafted the contract.

De bonis non administratis

de + bona, bonorum - goods + non + administrare - to administer, manage

Literally means "of goods not administered". Estate assets left unadministered when a prior executor cannot finish; a court may appoint an administrator de bonis non.

De bonis non administratis

When an executor dies, resigns, or is removed before finishing an estate, the court issues letters of administration d.b.n. so a new administrator can distribute the property that remains unadministered.

Ex contractu

ex + contractus, contractus - agreement

Literally means "out of contract". Arising out of a contract.

Ex gratia

ex + gratia, gratiae - grace, favor

Literally means "from grace". A payment or benefit made as a favor, without admission of liability.

OTHER RELATED TERMS

confer (*proferre*)
ministry (*administrare*)
distract (*contractus*)
gracious (*gratia*)

Factum

factum, facti - fact, deed

Literally means "an act". A deed or act.

Non est factum

non + factum, facti - fact, deed

Literally means "it is not my deed". A defense that a signed document is void because the signer was fundamentally mistaken about its nature or character and was not negligent.

Non est factum

In *Meridian Credit Union v. Vrankovic* (2013), the court rejected non est factum, holding it does not apply to a willfully blind signer.

Per stirpes

per + stirps, stirpis - stock, plant

Literally means "by the root". Estate shares pass down a family line.

Quantum (meruit)

quantum - how much + merere - to earn, deserve

Literally means "as much as he has earned". Recovery of the reasonable value of services when no enforceable contract governs payment to prevent unjust enrichment.

OTHER RELATED TERMS

benefactor (*factum*)
coefficient (*factum*)
extirpate (*stirps*)
merit (*merere*)

Quid pro quo

quis - who, which, something + pro

Literally means "something for something". An exchange of value.

Repudiation

repudium, repudii - divorce, rejection

A clear refusal to perform a contractual obligation before or when performance is due.

Scienter

scienter - skillfully, consciously

Literally means "consciously". A culpable state of mind; knowledge that a statement is false or that conduct wrongful, sometimes shown by reckless disregard.

Sine qua non

sine + quis - who, which, something + non

Literally means "without which not". Indicates an indispensable clause.

Quid pro quo

In the 1920s Teapot Dome scandal, Interior Secretary Albert Fall leased naval oil reserves in exchange for bribes.

OTHER RELATED TERMS

quiddity (*quid*)
impudent (*repudium*)
science (*scienter*)
conscious (*scienter*)

CONTRACT LAW

In a bustling Roman marketplace, a cloth merchant and a ship captain meet amidst the many voices around them. Fine linen is required for the captain's voyage east, and the merchant promises a shipment of it in a fortnight. They shake hands through mutual trust; however, the agreement is not carved in marble or written down in papyrus. Instead, it is binding because both individuals understand and intend the same thing.

As days pass, the merchant's supply lines are delayed by storms. He sends word to the captain honestly (instead of hiding this matter), offering to acquire linen from another trader (for that trader's profit instead of his own). This is bona fides, the good faith that comes with trust; honesty and fairness are as important as an official contract.

But what gave these individuals such motivations? Causa (cause): the merchant's hope for profit and the captain's need to sell goods abroad.

Yet why did these men stay bound to bona fides? Ratio (reason): In Rome, the obligatio was not an informal agreement. After an obligatio, if the merchant didn't make into reality what he had promised, the captain could drag him before the praetor, who would then declare, "Obligatio est iuris vinculum", "an obligation is a chain of law." Harsh, tiring, and long legal proceedings would ensue after.

In these ways, Roman contract law was established.

Assault

ad + salire - to leap, spring

An intentional act that causes a person to reasonably fear imminent harmful or offensive contact (no contact required).

Battery

batuere - to beat, strike

Intentional harmful or offensive physical contact with another.

Culpa lata

culpa, culpae - negligence + latus - wide, broad

Literally means "wide (gross) negligence". A severe departure from the required standard of care, often approaching recklessness.

Culpa levis

culpa, culpae - negligence + levis - light, thin

Literally means "light (ordinary) negligence". Failure to use the care a reasonable person would use in similar circumstances. A lesser degree of fault than gross negligence.

Battery

In *Garratt v. Dailey* (1955), the Washington Supreme Court held that battery intent is met if the actor knows with substantial certainty that contact will occur, even without a purpose to harm.

OTHER RELATED TERMS

insult (*salire*)
debate (*batuere*)
dilate (*latus*)
relief (*levis*)

Defamation

dis + fama, famae - rumor, report

Publication of a false statement of fact that harms another's reputation; typically requires fault and damages, with defenses such as truth or privilege.

Innuendo

in + nuere - to nod

Literally means "by hinting/nodding toward". An insinuation that implies a disparaging meaning; in defamation, an innuendo explains the defamatory meaning of ambiguous words.

Libel

libellus, libelli - little book

Written or otherwise fixed-form defamation (e.g. print or online).

Negligence

ne + legere - to choose, select

Failure to exercise reasonable care, causing damage. Elements of negligence are duty, breach, causation, and damages.

Libel

In *New York Times Co. v. Sullivan* (1964), the U.S. Supreme Court held that public officials must prove "actual malice", which is knowledge of falsity or reckless disregard for the truth, to recover for libel.

OTHER RELATED TERMS

famous (*fama*)
nuance (*nuere*)
librarian (*libellus*)
election (*legere*)

Novus actus interveniens

novus - new + actus, actus - act, deed + intervenire - to come between

Literally means "a new act intervening". An independent, unforeseeable event that breaks causation and may relieve the original defendant of liability.

Nuisance

nocere - to hurt, harm

An unreasonable interference with another's use of land.

Privacy

privus - one's own, individual

Protection against intrusion, public disclosure of private facts, false light, and appropriation of name or likeness.

Res ipsa loquitur

res, rei - thing + ipse - itself + loqui - to speak

Literally means "the thing speaks for itself". Allows an inference of negligence when the event would not ordinarily occur without negligence, the instrumentality was under the defendant's control, and the plaintiff did not contribute.

Res ipsa loquitur

In *Ybarra v. Spangard* (1994), a patient injured while unconscious could invoke res ipsa loquitur against multiple medical defendants, who then had to explain their care.

OTHER RELATED TERMS

innovate (*novus*)
innocuous (*nocere*)
deprive (*privus*)
colloquial (*loqui*)

Respondeat superior

re + spondere - to answer + superior - higher

Literally means "let the master answer". Employer vicarious liability for an employee's torts committed within the scope of employment.

Restitutio ad integrum

restitutio, restitutionis - reinstatement + ad + integer - untouched, whole

Literally means "restoration to original position". Principle that damages should place the injured party as nearly impossible in the pre-wrong position.

Strict

stringere - to draw tight

Liability imposed without proof of fault. Common for abnormally dangerous activities and some product claims.

Vicarious

vicis, vicis - change, succession, exchange

Liability for another person's act based on a legal relationship (e.g. employer and employee, or partners).

Strict

In *Rylands v. Fletcher* (1868), the defendant constructed a water reservoir, which leaked through old mine shafts and flooded the neighbor's mine, for which the House of Lords imposed strict liability.

OTHER RELATED TERMS

spouse (*spondere*)
integral (*integer*)
prestige (*stringere*)
vice (*vicis*)

TORT LAW

One day, a boy in ancient Athens decided to borrow his neighbor's clay jug to carry water from a well. On his way home, he tripped over a rock and dropped it, shattering it into many fragments. The neighbor wanted a replacement jug from the boy, while the boy insisted that he "didn't mean to break it."

When the matter reached the elders, they quoted Aristotle's words in Nicomachean Ethics, stating that a wrong is not just erased because it was unintentional. The jug is still broken and the neighbor still has no water on account of the broken jug. Aristotle argued that the doer of harm must restore what was lost, not because the harmer is a wicked person, but because fairness rules that the harmer owes the victim what the victim lost. The boy brought a new jug the next day to his neighbor.

Tort law was inspired by Roman examples like this, due to the fact that restoration as close to before the incident was the end goal; blame and excuses were only effective to a certain point.

Appurtenance

ad + pertinere - to belong to

A right or thing attached to and passing with the land.

Bona vacantia

bona, bonorum - goods + vacare - to be empty, vacant

Literally means "ownerless goods". Property with no owner that passes to the state, subject to statutes allowing later claims.

Conveyance

cum + via, viae - road, path

The transfer of title or an interest in property. Usually accomplished by a deed that identifies the parties and property and recorded to give notice.

Dominium

dominium, dominii - rule, ownership

Literally means "ownership". Full ownership of property with rights to use, enjoy, and dispose; comparable to a fee simple absolute.

Conveyance

The Statute of Frauds (1677) in England required transfers of interests in land to be in writing and signed.

OTHER RELATED TERMS

retention (*pertinere*)
vacation (*vacare*)
convey (*via*)
dominate (*dominium*)

Fieri facias

fieri - to become + facere - to cause, do, make

Literally means "that you cause to be done". A writ directing a proper officer to levy and sell a judgment debtor's property to satisfy a money judgment.

Fructus industriales

Under the doctrine of emblements, a tenant may harvest annual crops (fructus industriales) planted before the tenancy ends.

Fructus naturales/ industriales

fructus, fructus - fruit

Literally means "natural/industrial fruits". Naturales are products of land without human labor; part of the realty. Industriales (emblements) are annual cultivated crops treated as personal property; a tenant may reenter to harvest after transfer or lease end.

Hypotheca

hypotheca, hypothecae - pledge, security

Literally means "pledge". A non-possessory security right over property.

In rem

in - against + res, rei - thing

Literally means "against the thing". A proceeding directed at property; the judgment fixes rights in the property and binds all claimants.

OTHER RELATED TERMS

fiat (*fieri*)
frugal (*fructus*)
realistic (*res*)
surreal (*res*)

Lease

laxare - to loosen

A grant of the right to possess and use property for a term in exchange for rent.

Lex situs

lex, legis - law + situs, situs - situation, position

Literally means "law of the place". The law of the location governing property.

Mortgage

mors, mortis - death

A security interest in real property to secure a debt, enforceable by foreclosure on default. Historically a "dead pledge": if unpaid, the land was lost; if paid, the pledge ended.

Nemo dat quod non habet

nemo, neminis - no one + dare - to give + quis - who, which + non + habere - to have

Literally means "no one gives what he does not have". A transferee takes no better title than the transferor; a buyer from a thief gets no title, so the original owner's rights prevail.

Nemo dat quod non habet

In *Guggenheim v. Lubell* (1991), the museum was allowed to seek return of stolen art from a good-faith purchaser. A thief cannot pass a good title.

OTHER RELATED TERMS

leash (*laxare*)
website (*situs*)
immortal (*mors*)
prohibit (*habere*)

Probate

probare - to try, test, prove

The court process of proving a will and administering an estate.

Res derelictae

res, rei - thing + derelinquere - to leave behind

Literally means "things abandoned". Property intentionally discarded by the owner.

Riparian

ripa, ripae - bank, shore

Pertaining to land adjoining a natural watercourse or lake; riparian owners have rights to reasonable use and access to the water, subject to the equal rights of other owners and public regulation.

Terra nullius

terra, terrae - earth, land + nullus, nulli - no one

Literally means "land of no one". A doctrine treating territory as belonging to no state and open to acquisition, historically used to ignore indigenous title.

Terra nullius

In *Mabo v. Queensland* (1992), the High Court of Australia rejected terra nullius and recognized native title.

OTHER RELATED TERMS

proofread (*probare*)
reliquary (*derelinquere*)
annul (*nullus*)
captivate (*capere*)

PROPERTY LAW

On a sunny day after a harsh storm in ancient Rome, a farmer noticed that what he thought to be his neighbor's goat had wandered into his olive grove. He tied it up to keep it safe, expecting someone to come and claim it. Days turned into weeks, and weeks into months; still no neighbor arrived. The goat grew fat on Roman olives and eventually bore kids of its own. After a year, Roman law said the goat was now the farmer's possession. This ruling was called "usucapio", where possessing a good for long can turn into ownership.

There is an idea today that "possession is 9/10ths of the law," showing how much property is part of law. Property, in many ways, is less about suddenly claiming something; rather, it can take time and patience to solidify ownership.

PUBLIC LAW

PUBLIC LAW CONSISTS OF THE FOLLOWING:

Administrative Law: How agencies make, enforce, and interpret rules. Covers delegations of authority, rule-making and adjudication, judicial review, and procedural safeguards under the APA and due process.

Criminal Law: Substantive definitions of offenses and defenses, grading and sentencing, and the constitutional constraints on investigation and prosecution.

Tax Law: Principles governing how income, transactions, and entities are taxed. Addresses statutory interpretation, timing and characterization of income and deductions, credits, and the administrative process of assessment and enforcement.

Employment Law: Regulation of the workplace: hiring, wages and hours, discrimination and retaliation, accommodation, workplace safety, leave entitlements, and collective bargaining and labor relations.

Constitutional Law: Structure and limits of governmental power. Includes separation of powers and federalism, individual rights, and standards of review.

Adjudication

ad + iudicare - to judge

Applying law to specific facts and issuing an order resolving the parties' rights.

Agency

agere - to act, set in motion

A government body created by law to administer and enforce statutes.

Compliance

complere - to fill up

Conformity with laws, regulations, permits, or orders, and the systems used to ensure it.

Deference

de + ferre - to bring, carry

Yielding of a court's or tribunal's judgment to another lawful authority, often an administrative agency, based on delegated authority or specialized expertise, such as accepting a reasonable interpretation of a statute or regulation.

Deference

In ***Loper Bright v. Raimondo*** (2024), the U.S. Supreme Court overruled Chevron deference and held that courts must interpret statutes independently rather than defer to agency views.

OTHER RELATED TERMS

misjudge (*iudicare*)
navigate (*agere*)
supplement (*complere*)
infer (*ferre*)

Enforcement

fortis - strong, powerful

Agency investigations and actions to compel compliance, including inspections, subpoenas, administrative orders, civil penalties, and referrals for prosecution.

Interpretive

inter

Explaining the meaning of existing regulations and statutes. Interpretive rules and guidance state the agency's view, and do not bind the public like legislative rules.

Licensing

licere - to be allowed, be lawful

Official permission issued by an agency to engage in a regulated activity, including initial issuance and renewal, often subject to conditions.

Mandamus

mandare - to command

Literally means "we command". A court writ ordering an official or agency to perform a clear, nondiscretionary duty.

Licensing

Since 1994, the Federal Communications Commission (FCC) has assigned wireless spectrum licenses by auction, allocating airwaves for mobile networks.

OTHER RELATED TERMS

fortress (*fortis*)
interception (*inter*)
leisure (*licet*)
command (*mandare*)

Notice

noscere - to know

Formal notification of proposed or pending agency action that triggers the right to comment or a hearing. In rulemaking it announces the proposal and legal authority; in adjudication it identifies the issues and timing.

Promulgation

pro - forth + mulgere - to milk

Official publication of a regulation so it has legal effect (i.e. bringing it forth into force).

Provision

pro + videre - to see

A specific clause or section in a statute, regulation, or order. Provisions create duties, rights, exceptions, definitions, or procedures.

Regulation

regulare - to control by rule

A binding rule issued by an agency under delegated authority that has the force of law. Typically adopted through notice-and-comment and subject to judicial review.

Regulation

The Food and Drug Administration (FDA) issues regulations that set safety and labeling standards for foods, drugs, and medical devices, including premarket approval for new drugs.

OTHER RELATED TERMS

notation (*noscere*)
emulsion (*mulgere*)
revision (*videre*)
irregular (*regulare*)

Rulemaking

regula, regulae - rule, straight piece of wood

The process for creating, amending, or repealing regulations, usually through notice and comment.

Sanction

sancire - to decree, devote

A penalty or coercive measure to enforce compliance; it can also mean official approval. Examples include fines, license suspension, contempt orders, case dismissal, or, in international law, trade or financial restrictions.

Ultra vires

ultra - beyond + vis, viris - strength, power

Literally means "beyond the powers". Refers to actions taken by a person or group that goes beyond the scope of their legal powers.

Validation

valere - to be well, strong

Confirmation that a rule or action is legally effective and properly adopted.

Ultra vires

In ***Youngstown Sheet & Tube Co. v. Sawyer*** (1952), the Supreme Court held the President lacked authority to seize the steel mills, an action beyond his power without congressional authorization.

OTHER RELATED TERMS

regiment (*regula*)
saint (*sancire*)
violence (*vis*)
valedictorian (*valere*)

In a crowded Roman forum around 450 BCE, children wove through the crowd to the front, where they could literally touch words that were etched in bronze. These were the Twelve Tables, laws that were no longer censored from the public by patricians, but fixed and open for all to see. For the first time, an ordinary citizen could point to a tablet and state that "the law says so." This set the stage for law in writing.

Nowadays, when a city posts rules of driving online, or a federal agency must publish new regulations in the Federal Register, citizens cannot argue with laws, and the government can't hide in the shadows. They need them displayed, whether on bronze, parchment, or a PDF. The Twelve Tables demonstrate that a main goal of administrative law is to provide accessibility and transparency, for both citizens and the government that serves them.

Actus Reus

actus - act, action + reus - guilty

Literally means "guilty act". The prohibited conduct or omission that constitutes a crime.

Alibi

alius - other + ibi - there

Evidence that the accused was elsewhere when the crime occurred.

Arraignment

ad + ratio, rationis - calculation, account

The first court appearance where the charges are read and a plea is entered.

Capias Mittimus

capere - to take hold + mittere - to send

Literally means "you shall take, we send". A writ directing law enforcement to arrest a person and commit them to custody, typically to secure appearance or enforce a court order (e.g. failure to appear or probation violation).

Actus reus

In ***Robinson v. California*** (1962), the Court held that a state cannot criminalize the status of addiction, and that criminal liability requires conduct (actus reus), not mere condition.

OTHER RELATED TERMS

ambiguity (*actus*)
alienate (*alius*)
ratify (*ratio*)
commission (*mittere*)

Conviction

cum + vincere - to conquer

A formal finding of guilt by verdict or plea.

Corpus delicti

corpus, corporis - body + delictum, delicti - crime, offense

Literally means "body of the crime". Independent proof that a crime occurred.

Doli incapax

dolus, doli - trick, wrong + incapax, incapaxis - incapable

Literally means "incapable of wrong". Common-law presumption that young children lack criminal capacity; still recognized in some jurisdictions (e.g. Australia), but not used in U.S. criminal law.

Ex post facto

ex + post + factum, facti - fact, deed

Literally means "from a thing done afterward". A retroactive criminal law that disadvantages the accused.

Doli incapax

In *RP v The Queen* (2016), the High Court reaffirmed that for children aged 10–14 the prosecution must prove they knew their act was seriously wrong, not merely naughty.

OTHER RELATED TERMS

convince (*vincere*)
delinquent (*delictum*)
sedulous (*dolus*)
incapacity (*incapax*)

In dubio pro reo

in + dubium, dubii - doubt + pro + reus, rei - defendant, accused, culprit

Literally means "when in doubt (rule) for the accused". Doubt is resolved in the defendant's favor.

Lex talionis

lex, legis - law + talio, talionis - retaliation

Literally means "law of retaliation". An ancient principle of proportionate punishment ("eye for an eye") that today informs proportional sentencing, not a justification for private retaliation or crime.

Mens Rea

mens, mentis - mind + rea - guilty

Literally means "guilty mind". The mental state required for a crime.

Nolle prosequi

nolle - to be unwilling + prosequi - to pursue

Literally means "to not wish to pursue". A prosecutor's formal dismissal of charges.

Mens rea

The Model Penal Code (1962) defined four mental states (purposely, knowingly, recklessly, and negligently), standardizing mens rea.

OTHER RELATED TERMS

dubious (*dubium*)
legitimate (*lex*)
comment (*mens*)
sequence (*prosequi*)

Nolo contendere

nolle - to be unwilling + contendere - to stretch

Literally means "I do not wish to contend". A "no contest" plea treated like a guilty plea for sentencing; waives trial rights without admitting guilt.

Non bis in idem

non + bis - twice + in + idem - the same

Literally means "not twice in the same (thing)". The rule against double jeopardy (i.e. being punished twice for the same crime).

Non compos mentis

non + compos, compotis - mastery + mens, mentis - mind

Literally means "not master of one's mind". Used to denote lack of mental capacity to understand or manage one's affairs.

Nullum crimen sine lege

nullus, nulli - no one + crimen, criminis - punishment, indictment + sine + lex, legis - law

Literally means "no punishment without law". No criminal liability without a prior law defining the offense.

Non bis in idem

In ***Gamble v. United States*** (2019), the U.S. Supreme Court reaffirmed that state and federal governments may each prosecute the same conduct without violating double jeopardy.

OTHER RELATED TERMS

pretentious (*contendere*)
balance (*bis*)
impossible (*compos*)
incriminate (*crimen*)

CRIMINAL LAW

When Gaius, a young Roman merchant, was caught cheating his clients with false weights (courtesy of some witnesses), the consequences he faced were very unlike the punishments we face today. Rome had no huge prisons or tall walls to contain those who are guilty. Instead, the law only had a few options. Gaius could be fined, stripping him of almost everything he owned and leaving him dependent on the mercy and hospitality of friends or family. Gaius might also lose his rights. Infamia, which took away a man's voice in court, could stop him from holding office and make him lose his social position.

However, the worst penalty was exile. One that was cast away from Rome meant that they were taken away from one's patria, from the streets where he had traded, from the forums where he had debated, and from the temples where his ancestors had prayed. Life somewhere else would allow one to survive but not to belong; a Roman without Rome was like a captive on a boat, perpetually alien.

As Gaius contemplated his fate, he realized that the crime itself was very temporary, only a small urge of greed, but the punishment, from financial devastation to social downfall to exile, would stay for eternity. Without prisons, Rome had created a sense of iustitia (justice) that completely took away one's place in society, showing that sometimes the most severe shackles on a crime-committer were wielded by the hand of law.

Ad valorem

ad - according to + valor, valoris - economic value, valor

Literally means "according to value". A tax assessed based on value of property or a transaction.

Amortization

ad + mors, mortis - death

Gradual extinguishment by paying down a loan in scheduled installments until the balance is zero, or by writing off an intangible asset over time until its cost basis is fully recovered for tax or accounting.

Assessment

assidere - to sit beside

The official determination of value or tax due by a taxing authority.

Audit

audire - to hear, listen

Examination of records and returns to verify accuracy and compliance, conducted by a tax authority or independent auditors.

Ad valorem

VAT is an ad valorem consumption tax that applies a percentage rate to the value of goods and services.

OTHER RELATED TERMS

valuable (*valor*)
mortician (*mors*)
assess (*sedere*)
obedient (*audire*)

Avoidance

vacare - to be empty, vacant

Arranging affairs to minimize tax within the law, distinct from evasion. Common methods include timing income and deductions, choosing entity form, deferral, and using credits or exclusions.

Avoidance

IRC v. Duke of Westminster (1936) affirmed that a taxpayer may lawfully arrange affairs to reduce tax, a principle later narrowed by anti-avoidance doctrines like *Ramsay*.

Capital

caput, capitis - head

Wealth invested or used to produce income. In tax law, refers to capital assets and capital expenditures added to basis, with gains or losses on disposition and rates affected by holding period.

Collection

cum + legere - to collect

Actions to collect assessed tax, such as liens, levies, offsets, and installment agreements, with interest and penalties accruing.

Credit

credere - to trust, believe

An amount that reduces tax liability dollar for dollar. Credits may be nonrefundable or refundable.

OTHER RELATED TERMS

evacuate (*vacare*)
biceps (*caput*)
elite (*legere*)
miscreant (*credere*)

Deduction

de + ducere - to lead

An amount subtracted from income to compute taxable income.

Depreciation

de + pretium, pretii - price

Deducting the cost of tangible property over its useful life. Reduces basis and spreads recovery over time.

Ejusdem generis

idem - the same + genus, generis - origin, kind

Literally means "of the same kind". When general words follow specific ones, the general words are limited to the same class as the specifics.

Estate

status, status - state or condition, position

All property and interests owned at death, subject to administration and distribution by will or intestacy.

Deduction

In *Simon v. Commissioner* (2d Cir. 1995), professional violinists were allowed to depreciate antique Tourte bows used in performance, even though the bows' market value increased, because they suffered wear and tear in business use.

OTHER RELATED TERMS

ductile (*ducere*)
praise (*pretium*)
generational (*genus*)
distant (*status*)

Evasion

e/ex + vadere - to go, walk

Illegal nonpayment or underpayment of tax through fraud, such as concealing income or assets, inflating deductions, or using sham entities. Punishable by civil penalties and criminal charges.

Post mortem

post + mors, mortis - death

Literally means "after death". Occurring after death; often used for estate administration and tax elections made by the personal representative (e.g. portability election, alternate valuation).

Refund

re + fundere - to pour

Repayment of overpaid tax. Obtained by filing a return or refund within limitation periods.

Situs

situs, situs - situation, position

Literally means "location". The place that determines tax jurisdiction.

Situs

Most states use destination-based sales for tax sourcing, so the tax situs is where the buyer receives the goods.

OTHER RELATED TERMS

pervasive (*vadere*)
murrain (*mors*)
fusion (*fundere*)
situation (*situs*)

TAX LAW

In a sunny, Roman province with dusty streets, clay houses, and bustling markets, among the crowds is the publicanus, the Roman tax collector, with not only a ledger and quill, but also a mental count of numbers of people. To hold this position meant to hold power, but with a risk.

The Roman state did not send its own officials to collect taxes. Instead, it auctioned this duty to the highest bidder, which was usually a wealthy equestrian (equite, the second highest tier in Roman society consisting of those who worked their way up to a wealthy position). The winner paid Rome a large sum first, essentially pre-purchasing the province's tax revenue. From there on out, every transaction and levy on citizens he finds becomes both an opportunity and a risk of judgment and luck. Each coin taken from citizens beyond the initial tribute that the equite paid was immediately profit, but if the equite couldn't gather more money than what he initially paid, he personally lost money.

Walking through the streets, the publicanus had to face both compliance with his orders and resentment, sometimes violent. In Judea, local inhabitants often regarded publicani with suspicion or hostility. Tax collectors were usually local themselves, which made their role both morally and socially complicated. This is shown in historical texts, including the New Testament.

Being a publicanus required a resilient combination of wealth, courage, and pragmatism. It leveraged law and accounting, business and human interaction, understandings of local customs, and the balance between greed and duty to the people. For those who succeeded, it provided influence and profit; for those who failed, ruin and social disdain became inevitable. In this way, tax collection in the Roman Empire was as much a test of character as it was of numbers.

Benefits

bene - well + facere - to do

Non-wage compensation such as health-insurance or retirement plans.

Classification

classis, classis - division, fleet

Determining a worker's legal status (e.g. employee vs independent contractor, exempt vs non-exempt), which sets rights, benefits, and employer obligations; misclassification can deny protections and trigger penalties.

Compensation

cum + pendere - to hang, weigh, pay

Wages and other pay for work.

Discrimination

dis + cernere - to distinguish, separate

Adverse treatment based on a protected characteristic (e.g. race, color, religion, sex, national origin, age 40+, disability, genetic information).

Discrimination

In ***Bostock v. Clayton County*** (2020), the U.S. Supreme Court held that Title VII's ban on discrimination "because of sex" protects gay and transgender employees.

OTHER RELATED TERMS

benevolent (*bene*)
classroom (*classis*)
pension (*pendere*)
secret (*cernere*)

Employment

plicare - to fold

The legal relationship between employer and employee. Often "at will" unless altered by contract, statute, civil service rules, or a collective bargaining agreement.

Exemption

ex + emere - to buy

An exclusion from coverage or requirements, such as minimum wage or overtime rules. usually determined by duties and salary criteria.

Grievance

gravis - heavy, painful

A formal employee or union complaint under workplace rules or a CBA (Collective Bargaining Agreement).

In pari delicto

in + par, paris - equal + delictum, delicti - fault, offense

Literally means "in equal fault". A defense barring recovery when both sides are equally responsible for the wrongdoing.

Grievance

In the 1960 Steelworkers Trilogy, the U.S. Supreme Court required courts to compel grievance arbitration under CBAs and to defer the arbitrator's award.

OTHER RELATED TERMS

implicit (*plicare*)
impromptu (*emere*)
gravity (*gravis*)
relinquish (*delictum*)

Per diem

per + dies, diei - day

Literally means "for each day". A daily allowance or rate for expenses or pay (e.g. travel meals and lodging).

Restructuring

re + struere - to build

Organizational changes affecting the workforce such as layoffs, reorganizations, role changes, or hours reductions.

Retaliation

retaliare - to pay back in kind

Adverse action because an employee engaged in protected activity (e.g. reporting unsafe conditions, filing a discrimination complaint, or cooperating in an investigation).

Safety

salus, salutis - health, prosperity

Workplace health and safety standards and compliance including hazard control, training, PE, and recordkeeping.

Restructuring

In 2022, Twitter's restructuring under Elon Musk included mass layoffs, and workers filed WARN Act lawsuits in California alleging lack of 60-day notice.

OTHER RELATED TERMS

meridian (*dies*)
instrument (*struere*)
salutorian (*salus*)
salvage (*salus*)

Seniority

senior - older

Priority based on length of service, often governing layoffs and recall, promotions and transfers, scheduling and overtime, and vacation bidding.

Tenure

tenere - to hold

A status providing ongoing appointment and job protection after a probationary period.

Termination

terminus, termini - boundary, end

The end of the employment relationship. Usually "at will" unless modified by contract, statute, or a collective bargaining agreement.

Union

unus - one

An organization that represents workers in collective bargaining over wages, hours, and other terms of employment. At certification, the union is the exclusive representative for the bargaining unit and administers the contract through grievances and arbitration.

Union

In *Jones & Laughlin Steel v. NLRB* (1937), the U.S. Supreme Court upheld the National Labor Relations Act (NLRA), securing workers' rights to organize and bargain collectively.

OTHER RELATED TERMS

senile (*senior*)
impertinent (*tenere*)
terminology (*terminus*)
unicorn (*unus*)

EMPLOYMENT LAW

In ancient Rome, the law treated slaves as property instead of as people. This dehumanization was demonstrated in even the very words they spoke. A slave's testimony in court was already untrustworthy; it could only be admitted if given under torture, a violent method used to force truth from someone who was considered incapable of honesty. However, some masters found a good way to leverage the Roman understanding of iustitia (justice). Good masters, whether they did this out of alignment with their moral compasses, pragmatism, or respect for the law, would sometimes grant freedom to a slave before a trial, which allowed them to testify equally and with less bias and fear of punishment. Suddenly, the testimony of a former slave became credible, and the scales of justice tipped in the opposite direction, even if only a little. In this small action, one can see the paradox of Roman law where society, which has this basis of violence, has a hope for the truth, even if twisted methods are employed to make it come out. For the slave, freedom from good owners changes their voice as silenced property, revealing that morals of good citizens were already starting to take place in society to defy even an oppressive legal system.

Amendment

ex + mendum, mendi - fault, physical blemish, error

A formal change to a constitution. In the U.S., amendments are proposed by two-thirds of Congress or a convention and ratified by three-fourths of the states.

Appellate

appellere - to address/summon

Relating to the review of a lower court's decision; focuses on legal error, applies standards of review, and is decided on the existing record.

Certiorari

certior - more certain

Literally means "to be more informed". A writ by which a higher court reviews a lower court's decision.

Commerce

cum + merx, mercis - merchandise

In U.S. constitutional law, this refers to the Commerce Clause, which grants Congress power to regulate interstate and foreign commerce.

Certiorari

The Judiciary Act of 1925 made Supreme Court review largely discretionary through certiorari.

OTHER RELATED TERMS

emendation (*mendum*)
propeller (*appellere*)
concert (*certior*)
mercantilist (*merx*)

Delegation

de + legare - to send as an envoy, bequeath

Grant of lawmaking or enforcement authority to another body within defined limits.

Doctrine

docere - to show, teach

A legal principle or framework derived from cases, statutes, or constitutional text that sets elements and burdens, and guides later decisions.

Enumeration

e/ex + numerus, numeri - number

Listing specific powers or rights.

Federalism

foedus, foederis - treaty, league, alliance

Division of power between a central government and subnational units, with constitutional rules for competences, conflict resolution, finance, and cooperation.

Federalism

In *McCulloch v. Maryland* (1819), the U.S. Supreme Court affirmed Congress's implied powers and barred states from taxing the national bank.

OTHER RELATED TERMS

college (*legare*)
doctor (*docere*)
documentary (*docere*)
number (*numerus*)

Habeas corpus

habere - to have + corpus, corporis - body

Literally means "you should have the body". A writ to challenge the legality of detention and seek release; acts as a safeguard against unlawful imprisonment.

Habeas corpus

In 1861, President Lincoln suspended habeas corpus along key Union rail routes during the Civil War, sparking protests; Congress later authorized broader suspension in 1863.

Nationality

natio, nationis - birth, origin

Legal membership in a state. Acquired by birth, descent, or naturalization; distinct from residence. Confers rights and duties under the state's law.

Preamble

pre + ambulare - to walk

Introductory statement of a constitution's purposes and principles. Guides interpretation but is generally not enforceable on its own.

Preemption

pre + emere - to buy

Federal law displacing conflicting state law under the Supremacy Clause (U.S. Specific).

OTHER RELATED TERMS

incorporate (*corpus*)
renaissance (*natio*)
ambulance (*ambulare*)
premium (*emere*)

Privilege

privus - one's own, individual + lex, legis - law

A special legal right or immunity.

Supremacy

supremus - highest

The principle that the constitution is the highest law and that valid national law prevails over conflicting subnational law.

Ubi jus ibi remedium

ubi - where + ius, iuris - law, right + ibi - there + remedium, remedii - remedy, cure

Literally means "where there is a right there is a remedy". Courts should provide a remedy for violation of a legal right.

Veto

vetare - to forbid, prohibit

The constitutional power of an executive to refuse assent to a bill, preventing it from becoming law unless the legislature overrides under constitutional rules.

Supremacy

In *Cooper v. Aaron* (1958), the U.S. Supreme Court held that state officials must comply with federal court orders. Under the Supremacy Clause, the U.S. Constitution and the Supreme Court's interpretations are binding on the states.

OTHER RELATED TERMS

enterprise (*privus*)
summit (*supremus*)
survival (*supremus*)
medicine (*remedium*)

CONSTITUTIONAL LAW

In the Roman Forum, a citizen stepped forward, challenging a magistrate's ruling that he believed violated his rights. He used provocatio, the right to appeal, to show the court that even the magistrate had limits to his powers by law. Nearby, tribunes debated with consuls over a new levy of taxes. This action of the tributes attempted to protect the interests of the plebeians against the ambitions of the patricians. A jurist, hearing the argument, raised his voice for all to hear, quoting "salus populi suprema lex esto," "the welfare of the people shall be the supreme law" in favor of the plebeians, showing that law serves the public, not the rulers.

Across the city, in a quieter area, senators debated treaties and trade, leveraging ius gentium, "the law of nations," to create interactions with foreign peoples. They understood that fairness and order could create a balance on the scales that centuries later would inspire constitutional protections of equality and international relations.

Centuries after these events, the Framers of the U.S. Constitution had to face their own challenges, such as balancing federal and state powers, protecting individual rights, and making sure that no branch of government would be unchecked. Each clause of the Bill of Rights, freedom of speech, the right to a fair trial, or due process, brought in Roman law. The Constitution created the connections between authority, rights, and the common good from the ancient Republic to the modern one.

INTERNATIONAL LAW

International law governs relations among states and international organizations. It allocates authority, regulates cooperation and conflict, and supplies common rules for borders, seas, trade, investment, the environment, human rights, and the use of force.

Understanding these terms can aid your comprehension of treaties, court judgements, UN resolutions, and diplomatic correspondence.

Examples of International Law:

- Cession
- Expropriation
- Mare librum
- Persona non grata

Annexation

ad + nectere - to tie, bind

Incorporation of territory into another state. Modern international law bars acquisition of territory by force, so annexations lack lawful effect and are often not recognized.

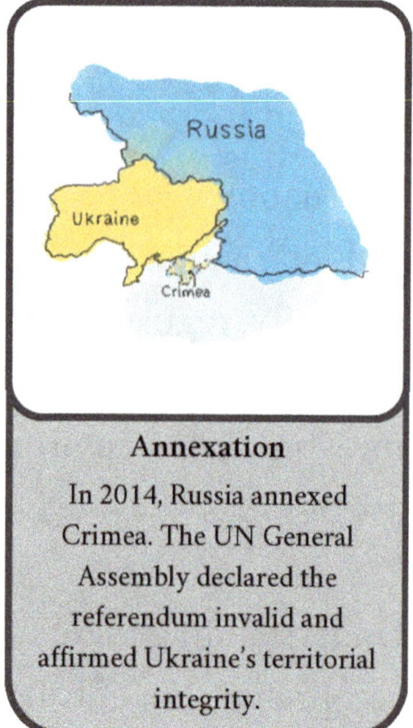

Annexation

In 2014, Russia annexed Crimea. The UN General Assembly declared the referendum invalid and affirmed Ukraine's territorial integrity.

Asylum

asylum, asyli - sanctuary

Protection a state grants to a person fleeing persecution that allows them to remain and not be returned. Grounded in the non-refoulement principle and may be territorial (in the country) or diplomatic (in embassies).

Bilateral

bis - two + latus, lateris - the side

Involving two states.

OTHER RELATED TERMS

connect (*nectere*)
nexus (*nectere*)
ancestor (*cedere*)
recession (*cedere*)

Cession

cedere - to go away, yield

Transfer of territory or sovereignty, typically through a treaty. Sovereignty passes with consent of the states.

Custom

consuescere - to become accustomed to

Customary international law formed by accepted general and consistent state practice.

Diplomacy

diploma, diplomatis - certificate of privileges

Management of international relations through negotiation.

Erga omnes

erga - towards + omnis, omnis - all

Literally means "towards all". Obligations owed to the international community as a whole.

Expropriation

ex + proprius - one's own

State taking of private property. Lawful takings require a public purpose, non-discrimination, due process, and compensation. Indirect or "creeping" expropriation occurs when measures effectively deprive an owner of use or value.

Erga omnes

In *Barcelona Traction* (ICJ, 1970), the Court recognized certain obligations (e.g. prohibitions on genocide, slavery, and racial descrimination) as erga omnes, meaning any state may invoke their breach.

OTHER RELATED TERMS

costume (*consuescere*)
bus (*omnis*)
omniscient (*omnis*)
propriety (*proprius*)

Extraterritoriality

extra + terra, terrae - earth, land

Application of a state's laws or jurisdiction beyond its territory.

Hostis humani generis

hostis, hostis - enemy + humanus - human + genus, generis - kind, origin

Literally means "enemy of mankind". A universal enemy subject to jurisdiction by all states. Historically meant for pirates.

Intervention

inter + venire - to come

Interference by one state in another state's affairs.

Iura novit curia

ius, iuris - law, right + noscere - to know + curia, curiae - senate, court

Literally means "the court knows the law". A court may apply the correct law even if the parties do not plead it.

Extraterritoriality

Under GDPR Article 3, EU data rules apply to companies worldwide if they offer goods or services to, or monitor the behavior of, people in the EU.

OTHER RELATED TERMS

terrace (*terra*)
hostile (*hostis*)
convention (*venire*)
cognisant (*noscere*)

Ius ad bellum

ius, iuris - law, right + ad + bellum, belli - war

Literally means "right to war". Law governing when states may resort to force.

Ius cogens

ius, iuris - law, right + cogere - to gather, compel

Literally means "compelling law". Peremptory norms from which no derogation (setting aside a rule) is permitted, meaning these are fundamental rules that states cannot violate through agreements or customary practice.

Ius gentium

ius, iuris - law, right + gens, gentis - tribe, nation

Literally means "law of nations". International law governing relations among states.

Ius in bello

ius, iuris - law, right + in + bellum, belli - war

Literally means "law in war". Law governing conduct during armed conflict.

Ius ad bellum

The UN Charter (1945) bars the use of force in international relations except for self-defense under Article 51 or when authorized by the Security Council.

OTHER RELATED TERMS

belligerent (*bellum*)
rebellion (*bellum*)
generalize (*gens*)
indigenous (*gens*)

Mare liberum

mare, maris - sea + liber - free

Literally means "free sea (freedom of the seas)". The high seas are not owned by any state; all states may carry out actions subject to international law.

Mare librum

The UN Convention on the Law of the Sea (1982) codifies high-seas freedoms like navigation and fishing, an idea from Hugo Grotius's *Mare Librum.*

Multilateral

multus - many + latus, lateris - the side

Involving three or more states.

Neutrality

neuter - neither

Status of nonparticipation in an armed conflict with related rights and duties. Neutrals must avoid assisting belligerents and prevent use of their territory.

Occupation

ob + capere - to take, capture

Effective control of territory without sovereignty transfer. The occupant acts as a temporary administrator under the law or occupation, must maintain public order and respect existing laws, and may not annex or exploit resources unlawfully.

OTHER RELATED TERMS

submarine (*mare*)
libertarianism (*liber*)
neutron (*neuter*)
reception (*capere*)

Pacta sunt servanda

pactum, pacti - agreement +
servare - to save

Literally means "agreements must be kept". Treaties in force are binding and must be performed in good faith.

Pacta sunt servanda
Article 26 of the Vienna Convention on the Law of Treaties (1969) codifies that every treaty in force is binding on the parties and must be performed in good faith.

Passport

passus, passus - step, pace +
portus, portus - harbor

Government document that identifies the bearer and permits international travel.

Persona non grata

persona, personae - person +
non + gratia, gratiae -
goodwill, favor, esteem

Literally means "an unwelcome person". A diplomat declared unacceptable by the host state and required to be recalled.

Rebus sic stantibus

res, rei - thing + sic - thus +
stare - to stand

Literally means "thus with things standing". Doctrine allowing treaty termination or suspension due to a fundamental change of circumstances.

OTHER RELATED TERMS

patio (*pactum*)
conserve (*servare*)
opportunity (*portus*)
parsonage (*persona*)

Recognition

re + cognoscere - to learn, become acquainted with

Acknowledgment of a state, government, or status.

Refugee

re + fugere - to flee

A person outside their country with a well-founded fear of persecution who cannot or will not return.

Sovereignty

super

Supreme authority within one's own territory and independence from external control.

Uti possidetis, ita possideatis

uti - as + possidere - to hold + ita - thus, so

Literally means "as you possess, so may you possess". Doctrine fixing new international borders along existing administrative lines at independence to promote stability.

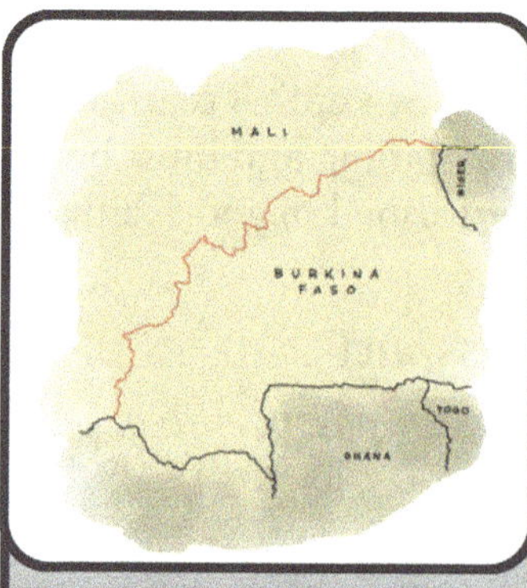

Uti possidetis, ita possideatis

In *Frontier Dispute (Burkina Faso/Mali)* (1986), the ICJ confirmed that at independence colonial administrative boundaries become international borders under uti possidetis.

OTHER RELATED TERMS

noble (*cognoscere*)
centrifuge (*fugere*)
soprano (*super*)
possessive (*possidere*)

Imagine walking through a courtroom in Paris, Buenos Aires, or Tokyo. Although each of these places are separated by continents, the law of the Roman Republic is demonstrated in each verdict. Roman law is in the Corpus Juris Civilis and is practiced for centuries in the Roman Forum. It includes contracts, property rights, and legalities that became the basis of modern civil law. France adopted these ideas in the Napoleonic Code, which influenced Argentina's legal system. Germany incorporated Roman doctrines into the Bürgerliches Gesetzbuch, and Japan used aspects of its civil code in both German and French law. It's remarkable that a Republic that vanished over two thousand years ago still impacts governance of nations around the world today, showing that quality laws and preservation can endure much, much longer than empires.

Beyond courts and codes, Rome dealt with its neighbors in a language of rites and leverage. In the early Republic, fetial priests carried demands for redress; if none came after the set days, they declared a just war. Peace took shape as foedera (formal treaties sworn with oaths). On the field a commander could promise terms by sponsio, but the people might refuse to honor them, as after the Caudine Forks. Defeated enemies sometimes chose deditio in fidem (a surrender into Rome's good faith), placing themselves under Rome's protection while Rome fixed their new standing as allies, client kings, or provinces. The words stayed courteous as power tilted: embassies remained inviolate under the ius gentium, yet settlements asked for tribute, garrisons, and obsides, the hostages described throughout *Caesar's De Bello Gallico.* Over time the web tightened. Italian allies gained citizenship after the Social War, client realms were annexed, and provincial charters set taxes and courts. The forms changed, but the pattern held: promises made in public, enforced by capacity, remembered in formulas that later jurists would call the law of nations.

PROCEDURAL LAW

Procedural law provides the framework for adjudication that ensures fair and reliable decisions. It defines how cases are presented, argued, and decided; standardizing the process in order to protect the law and the legal rights of people.

Court cases can be very daunting, as litigation has many moving parts. Learning these terms and phrases will help you understand the process and how cases are argued and decided.

Examples of Procedural Law:

- Ad hominem
- Non sequitur
- Quorum
- Subpoena

Ad hominem

ad + homo, hominis - person

Literally means "to the person". An attack on a person rather than the argument.

Ad ignorantiam

ad + ignorantia, ignorantiae - ignorance

Literally means "(appeal) to ignorance". A logical fallacy asserting a claim is true or false simply because it has not been proven otherwise.

Ad litem

ad + lis, litis - suit/lawsuit

Literally means "for the suit". Appointment to act in a case for someone unable to represent themselves.

Ad misericordiam

ad + misericordia, misericordiae - pity, compassion

Literally means "(appeal) to pity". A plea that relies on sympathy rather than proof.

Ad litem

Courts appoint a guardian ad litem to speak for the best interests of a child or incapacitated person in litigation, such as custody or settlement approvals.

OTHER RELATED TERMS

homage (*homo*)
ignoramus (*ignorantia*)
allege (*lis*)
misericord (*misericordia*)

Ad populum

ad + populus, populi - people

Literally means "(appeal) to the people". Arguing from popularity rather than evidence.

Affidavit

ad + fidus - faithful, loyal

Literally means "he made a pledge". A written statement sworn or affirmed before an authorized officer for use as evidence.

Amicus curiae

amicus - friend + curia, curiae - senate, court

Literally means "friend of the court". A nonparty submission that aids the court with legal analysis or broader consequences.

Audi alteram partem

audire - to hear + alter - other + pars, partis - part

Literally means "hear the other side". Each party must have timely notice and a fair opportunity to present and respond.

Ad populum
In *Sheppard v. Maxwell* (1966), the Supreme Court overturned Sam Sheppard's conviction after pervasive media coverage and a carnival atmosphere tainted the trial, showing that crowd sentiment is not evidence.

OTHER RELATED TERMS

popular (*populus*)
defiant (*fidus*)
amicable (*amicus*)
apartment (*pars*)

Coram non judice

coram - in the presence of + non + iudex, iudicis - judge

Literally means "not before a judge". Proceedings taken without proper jurisdiction and are considered invalid.

Credibility

credere - to believe

Worthiness of belief of a witness or evidence. Assessed by consistency, plausibility, bias, demeanor, prior statements, and corroboration.

De novo

de + novus - new

Literally means "from the beginning". A fresh determination as if not previously decided, used for certain appeals or reviews where the tribunal reconsiders issues without deference.

Deposition

deponere - to lay aside

Sworn out-of-court testimony recorded for later use.

Deposition

President Bill Clinton's civil deposition was under oath; misleading testimony led to a contempt sanction and helped set the stage for his impeachment.

OTHER RELATED TERMS

credence (*credere*)
creditor (*credere*)
novelist (*novus*)
deposit (*deponere*)

Discovery

dis - opposite of + cooperire - to cover up

Pretrial process for obtaining information, documents, and testimony from the other side.

Error in procedendo

error, erroris - error, wandering + in + procedere - to proceed, advance

Literally means "error in proceeding". A procedural error by the lower court.

Ex parte

ex + pars, partis - piece, par

Literally means "from one party". Action taken without the other party's participation or notice.

Ex relatione

ex + relatio, relationis - narration

Literally means "on behalf of". An action brought in the government's name on the information of a private relator.

Ex relatione
Under the False Claims Act, private whistleblowers file suit ex rel. in the name of the United States and may receive a share of any recovery.

OTHER RELATED TERMS

curfew (*cooperire*)
handkerchief (*cooperire*)
procession (*procedere*)
impartial (*pars*)

Functus officio

fungi - to perform, execute + officium, officii - office, duty

Literally means "having performed the office". Authority in the matter has ended.

Ignorantia juris non excusat

ignorantia, ignorantiae - ignorance + ius, iuris - law, right + non + excusare - to excuse, justify

Literally means "ignorance of the law does not excuse". Lack of knowledge of a law is not a defense to liability or a crime.

In absentia

in + absentia, absentiae - absence

Literally means "in absence". Proceedings conducted without the person present.

In camera

in + camera, camerae - room, chamber

Literally means "in the chamber". Proceedings or filings kept from public view.

Igorantia juris non excusat

Although the general rule remains that ignorance of the law is no defense, a narrow exception was recognized in *Lambert v. California* (1957): for a passive offense with no notice, lack of knowledge can excuse.

OTHER RELATED TERMS

officer (*officium*)
defunctive (*fungi*)
essential (*absentia*)
chamber (*camera*)

In flagrante delicto

in + flagrare - to be on fire + delictum, delicti - crime, offense

Literally means "while the crime is ablaze". Caught in the act of committing a crime. Used to justify immediate arrest or seizure.

In limine

in + limen, liminis - threshold, entrance

Literally means "at the threshold". A pretrial motion to decide admissibility of evidence.

In re

in + res, rei - thing, matter

Literally means "in the matter of". Used in case captions to for proceedings centered on a thing or status (e.g. probate, bankruptcy, guardianship).

Inter partes

inter + pars, partis - part, party

Literally means "between the parties". Proceedings involving and binding the opposing parties.

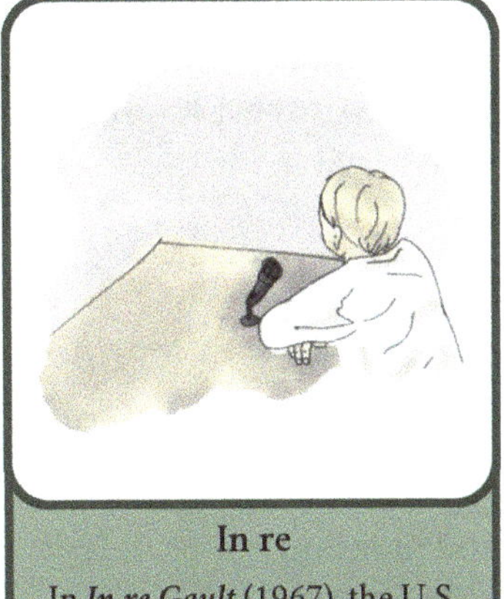

In re

In *In re Gault* (1967), the U.S. Supreme Court held that juveniles in delinquency cases have due process rights.

OTHER RELATED TERMS

flagrant (*flagrare*)
flamingo (*flagrare*)
sublime (*limen*)
internet (*inter*)

Inter vivos

inter + vivus - living

Literally means "between the living". A transfer or act made during life (e.g. "She set up an inter vivos trust to give the house to her son).

Joinder

iungere - to join together, unite

Joining multiple parties or claims in one case for efficiency and avoiding inconsistent judgements.

Lis pendens

lis, litis - suit/lawsuit + pendere - to hang

Literally means "suit pending". A recorded notice that litigation concerning real property is pending.

Locus standi

locus, loci - place + stare - to stand

Literally means "place of standing". The right to bring or participate in a case, requiring a sufficient interest or injury.

Locus standi

Lujan v. Defenders of Wildlife (1992) defined locus standi in U.S. courts as requiring injury in fact, causation, and redressability.

OTHER RELATED TERMS

vivid (*vivus*)
jugular (*iungere*)
pendulum (*pendere*)
allocate (*locus*)

Nemo judex in causa sua

nemo, neminis - no one + iudex, iudicis - judge + in + causa, causae - reason, case + suus - one's own

Literally means "no one is the judge in their own case". Requires an impartial decision-maker.

Nemo judex in causa sua

Pinochet (1999) set aside a House of Lords judgement for apparent bias due to a Law Lord's undisclosed ties to Amnesty International.

Non sequitur

non + sequi - to follow

Literally means "it does not follow". A conclusion that does not logically follow from the premises.

Notary

nota, notae - letter, note

A public officer authorized to authenticate documents and administer oaths.

Nunc pro tunc

nunc - now + pro + tunc - then

Literally means "now for then". An order entered now with retroactive effect to correct or reflect what should have occurred earlier.

OTHER RELATED TERMS

recuse (*causa*)
intrinsic (*sequi*)
connotation (*nota*)
quidnunc (*nunc*)

Obiter dictum

obiter - in passing + dicere - to say

Literally means "said in passing". Judicial remarks not essential to the decision.

Objection

ob - in front of, against + iacere - to throw

A formal protest to evidence or procedure.

Onus probandi

onus, oneris - burden, cargo + probare - to try, test, prove

Literally means "burden of proving". The obligation to prove a fact or claim.

Onus probandi

Woolmington v DPP (1935) called the prosecution's burden of proof the "golden thread" of criminal law: the state must prove guilt.

Pendete lite

pendere - to hang + lis, litis - lawsuit

Literally means "during litigation". Temporary orders while a case is pending; distinct from lis pendens, a recorded notice that litigation concerning real property is pending.

OTHER RELATED TERMS

dictator (*dicere*)
jet (*iacere*)
exonerate (*onus*)
pendant (*pendere*)

Per curiam

per + curia, curiae - court, senate

Literally means "through the court". An unsigned opinion issued in the court's name.

Post hoc ergo propter hoc

post + hic - this + ergo - therefore + propter - on account of

Literally means "after this therefore because of this". The fallacy that sequence alone implies causation. (e.g. "I failed a test an hour after making my bed, so making the bed caused the failure").

Precedent

prae + cedere - to go, march

A past decision that is binding or persuasive in later related cases.

Pro se

pro + se - oneself

Literally means "for oneself". Representing oneself without a lawyer.

Precedent

Although courts follow precedent, they can also overturn it when it is wrong and unworkable, shown by how ***Brown v. Board of Education*** (1954) overruled ***Plessy v. Ferguson*** (1896).

OTHER RELATED TERMS

curial (*curia*)
puny (*post*)
success (*cedere*)
unnecessary (*cedere*)

Quod erat demonstrandum (Q.E.D.)

qui - which + demonstrare - to show

Literally means "that which was to be shown". A notation indicating a proof is complete.

Quorum

qui - who

Literally means "of whom". The minimum number required.

Ratio decidendi

ratio, rationis - reason + decidere - to decide

Literally means "reason for deciding". The legal principle that controls the outcome.

Reductio ad absurdum

re + ductio, ductionis - leading away + ad + absurdus - absurd, nonsensical

Literally means "reduction to the absurd". Showing a claim leads to an absurd or contradictory result.

Quorum

In *United States v. Ballin* (1892), the U.S. Supreme Court ruled that the House can meet quorum by counting members who are present, even if they do not vote, which ended "disappearing quorum".

OTHER RELATED TERMS

monstrosity (*demonstrare*)
quibble (*qui*)
rationale (*ratio*)
surdism (*absurdus*)

Res gestae

res, rei - thing + gerere - to bear, wage

Literally means "things having been done". Events or statements so closely connected to an occurrence that they may be admitted as evidence.

Res judicata

res, rei - thing + iudicare - to judge

Literally means "a matter having been judged". After a final court judgment, the same parties are barred from relitigating the same claim or others arising from the same transaction

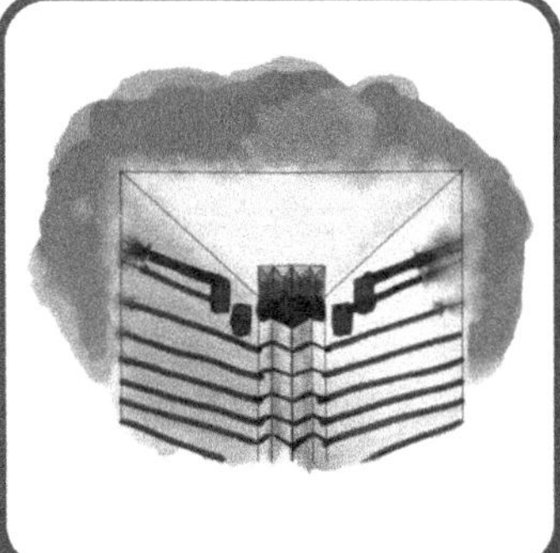

Res judicata

In *Federated Department Stores Inc. v. Moltie* (1981), the U.S. Supreme Court held that after a final judgement, the same parties cannot sue again on the same claim, even if the first decision was wrong.

Respondent

re + spondere - to pledge

The party responding to an appeal or petition.

Severance

se + parare - to prepare

Separating trials, claims, or defendants to avoid prejudice or for convenience and efficiency.

OTHER RELATED TERMS

gesture (*gerere*)
perjury (*iudicare*)
sponsor (*spondere*)
parade (*parare*)

Speculation

specere - to look, view

An inference or opinion not based on sufficient evidence.

Stare decisis

stare - to stand + decidere - to decide

Literally means "to stand by things decided". The doctrine of following precedent. Lower courts are bound by higher courts in the same system; departure requires a special justification.

Sua sponte

suus - its own + spons, spontis - free will

Literally means "of one's own accord". Action taken by the court without a request, such as raising jurisdiction or ordering additional briefing.

Sub judice

sub + iudex, iudicis - judge

Literally means "under a judge". A matter pending before the court (e.g. public officials may avoid comment while it is sub judice).

Stare decisis
Kimble v. Marvel (2015) applied stare decisis to keep the Brulotte rule that patent royalties cannot extend beyond the patent's expiration.

OTHER RELATED TERMS

spectrum (*specere*)
stage (*stare*)
stance (*stare*)
spontaneous (*spons*)

Subpoena

sub + poena - punishment, penalty

Literally means "under penalty". A court order to appear or produce evidence.

Subpoena
United States v. Nixon (1974) required the President to comply with a subpoena for Oval Office tapes.

Sub silentio

sub + silentium, silentii - silence

Literally means "under silence". A point resolved without express discussion.

Sustained

sub + tenere - to hold

The court agrees with an objection.

Vigilantibus non dormientibus iura subveniunt

vigilans, vigilantis - vigilant, alert + non + dormire - to sleep + ius, iuris - law, right + subvenire - to assist

Literally means "the law helps the vigilant, not the sleeping". Rights favor those who act to protect them.

OTHER RELATED TERMS

penalize (*poena*)
suffix (*sub*)
tennis (*tenere*)
surveillance (*vigilans*)

In the Roman courts, the drama of a procedure sometimes went against the drama of the law itself. When trials went badly and defeat looked inevitable, it was not unheard of for defendants to choose exile on themselves over a public loss that would lead to social devastation. Verres, for example, whose crimes were so egregious that Cicero's speeches of prosecution against him made him even more famous, fled Rome instead of facing the consequences of decided conviction. Even the judges were scrutinized (not unlike today); during a hard case, Cicero accused Mark Antony, the judge, of arriving to court drunk on the bench, which was written in his Philippics. In Rome, as in modern courts, procedure helped law determine how strategy, reputation, and credibility could tip the scales of justice.

This procedural structure, known as the formulary process, had two steps: 1. In iure: a magistrate would decide if the case was worth hearing; if it was relevant, the magistrate would write a formula for the judge 2. Apud iudicem: the judge, an ordinary appointed citizen, would use the formula and evidence to rule on the case. It is in step 2, apud iudicem, where Cicero would have delivered his strong orations to sway the judge. Before this procedural style, there was legis actiones (adopted during the institution of the Twelve Tables), which encouraged formalism to the point that a small mistake in wording could completely bring down an otherwise strong case. Over time, as Roman society became more flexible, its procedural systems became flexible as well. Cognitio extraordinaria, which came after the formulary process, gave most judicial power to an appointed magistrate that ruled over the whole case. The changes from citizen litigation to a more governmental and professional judiciary reveals how our modern society established procedural law from these new, Roman beginnings.

LIST OF TERMS

A fortiori (Latin: *a* + *fortis, forte* - strong)
A priori (Latin: *a* + *prior* - before)
Ab initio (Latin: *ab* + *initium, initii* - beginning)
Ab intestato (Latin: *ab* + *intestatus* - intestate, having made no will)
Acquisition (Latin: *ad* + *quaerere* - to seek, obtain)
Actio in personam (Latin: *actio, actionis* - action + *in* - against + *persona, personae* - person)
Actus Reus (Latin: *actus* - act, action + *reus* - guilty)
Ad hoc (Latin: *ad* + *hoc* - this)
Ad hominem (Latin: *ad* + *homo, hominis* - person)
Ad ignorantiam (Latin: *ad* + *ignorantia, ignorantiae* - ignorance)
Ad infinitum (Latin: *ad* + *infinitus* - endless, infinity)
Ad litem (Latin: *ad* + *lis, litis* - suit/lawsuit)
Ad misericordiam (Latin: *ad* + *misericordia, misericordiae* - pity, compassion)
Ad nauseam (Latin: *ad* + *nausea, nauseae* - seasickness)
Ad populum (Latin: *ad* + *populus, populi* - people)
Ad valorem (Latin: *ad* - according to + *valor, valoris* - economic value, valor)
Adjudication (Latin: *ad* + *iudicare* - to judge)
Adoption (Latin: *ad* + *optare* - to choose, wish)
Affidavit (Latin: *ad* + *fidus* - faithful, loyal)
Affiliate (Latin: *affiliare* - to adopt a son)
Agency (Latin: *agere* - to act, set in motion)
Alibi (Latin: *alius* - other + *ibi* - there)
Amendment (Latin: ex + *mendum, mendi* - fault, physical blemish, error)
Amicus curiae (Latin: *amicus* - friend + *curia, curiae* - senate, court)
Amortization (Latin *ad* + *mors, mortis* - death)

LIST OF TERMS

Animus (Latin: *animus, animi* - mind)
Annexation (Latin: *ad* + *nectere* - to tie, bind)
Annulment (Latin: *ad* + *nullus, nulli* - none, nothing)
Appellate (Latin: *appellere* - to address/summon)
Appurtenance (Latin: *ad* + *pertinere* - to belong to)
Arraignment (Latin: *ad* + *ratio, rationis* - calculation, account)
Assault (Latin: *ad* + *salire* - to leap, spring)
Assessment (Latin: *assidere* - to sit beside)
Asylum (Latin: *asylum, asyli* - sanctuary)
Audi alteram partem (Latin: *audire* - to hear + *alter* - other + *pars, partis* - part)
Audit (Latin: *audire* - to hear, listen)
Avoidance (Latin: *vacare* - to be empty, vacant)
Battery (Latin: *batuere* - to beat, strike)
Benefits (Latin: *bene* - well + *facere* - to do)
Bilateral (Latin: *bis* - two + *latus, lateris* - the side)
Bona fide (Latin: *bonus* - good + *fides, fidei* - faith)
Bona vacantia (Latin: *bona, bonorum* - goods + *vacare* - to be empty, vacant)
Capias Mittimus (Latin: *capere* - to take hold + *mittere* - to send)
Capital (Latin: *caput, capitis* - head)
Capital (Latin: *caput, capitis* - head)
Caveat emptor (Latin: *cavere* - to beware + *emptor, emptoris* - buyer)
Certiorari (Latin: *certior* - more certain)
Cession (Latin: *cedere* - to go away, yield)
Classification (Latin: *classis, classis* - division, fleet)
Cohabitation (Latin: *cum* + *habitare* - to live, dwell)
Collection (Latin: *cum* + *legere* - to collect)
Commerce (Latin: *cum* + *merx, mercis* - merchandise)
Compensation (Latin: *cum* + *pendere* - to hang, weigh, pay)
Compliance (Latin: *complere* - to fill up)

LIST OF TERMS

Consensus ad idem (Latin: *consensus, consensus* - agreement + *ad* + *idem* - the same)
Consideration (Latin: *cum* + *sidus, sideris* - star, constellation)
Consolidation (Latin: *cum* + *solidare* - to make solid)
Contra bonos mores (Latin: *contra* + *bonus* - good + *mos, moris* - custom, moral)
Contra proferentem (Latin: *contra* + *proferre* - to bring forward)
Conveyance (Latin: *cum* + *via, viae* - road, path)
Conviction (Latin: *cum* + *vincere* - to conquer)
Coram non judice (Latin: *coram* - in the presence of + *non* + *iudex, iudicis* - judge)
Corporation (Latin: *corpus, corporis* - body)
Corpus delicti (Latin: *corpus, corporis* - body + *delictum, delicti* - crime, offense)
Credibility (Latin: *credere* - to believe)
Credit (Latin: *credere* - to trust, believe)
Culpa lata (Latin: *culpa, culpae* - negligence + *latus* - wide, broad)
Culpa levis (Latin: *culpa, culpae* - negligence + *levis* - light, thin)
Custody (Latin: *custos, custodis* - guardian, protector)
Custom (Latin: *consuescere* - to become accustomed to)
De bonis non administratis (Latin: *de* + *bona, bonorum* - goods + *non* + *administrare* - to administer, manage)
De facto (Latin: *de* + *factum, facti* - fact, deed)
De jure (Latin: *de* - concerning + *ius, iuris* - law, right)
De minimis (non curat lex) (Latin: *de* + *minimus* - smallest + *non* + *curare* - to care + *lex, legis* - law)
De novo (Latin: *de* + *novus* - new)
Deduction (Latin: *de* + *ducere* - to lead)
Defamation (Latin: *dis* + *fama, famae* - rumor, report)
Deference (Latin: *de* + *ferre* - to bring, carry)
Delegation (Latin: *de* + *legare* - to send as an envoy, bequeath)

LIST OF TERMS

Deposition (Latin: *deponere* - to lay aside)
Depreciation (Latin: *de* - down + *pretium, pretii* - price)
Diplomacy (Latin: *diploma, diplomatis* - certificate of privileges)
Director (Latin: *dirigere* - to set right)
Discovery (Latin: *dis* - opposite of + *cooperire* - to cover up)
Discrimination (Latin: *dis* + *cernere* - to distinguish, separate)
Dividend (Latin: *dividere* - to separate)
Doctrine (Latin: *docere* - to show, teach)
Doli incapax (Latin: *dolus, doli* - trick, wrong + *incapax, incapaxis* - incapable)
Domicile (Latin: *domus, domi* - house + *colere* - to dwell)
Dominium (Latin: *dominium, dominii* - rule, ownership)
Ejusdem generis (Latin: *idem* - the same + *genus, generis* - origin, kind)
Emancipation (Latin: *e* + *manus, manus* - hand + *capere* - to take)
Employment (Latin: *plicare* - to fold)
Enforcement (Latin: *fortis* - strong, powerful)
Enumeration (Latin: *e/ex* + *numerus, numeri* - number)
Erga omnes (Latin: *erga* - towards + *omnis, omnis* - all)
Error in procedendo (Latin: *error, erroris* - error, wandering + *in* + *procedere* - to proceed, advance)
Estate (Latin: *status, status* - state or condition, position)
Evasion (Latin: *e/ex* + *vadere* - to go, walk)
Ex contractu (Latin: *ex* + *contractus, contractus* - agreement)
Ex gratia (Latin: *ex* + *gratia, gratiae* - grace, favor)
Ex parte (Latin: *ex* + *pars, partis* - piece, part)
Ex post facto (Latin: *ex* + *post* + *factum, facti* - fact, deed)
Ex relatione (Latin: *ex* + *relatio, relationis* - narration)
Exemption (Latin: *ex* + *emere* - to buy)
Expropriation (Latin: *ex* + *proprius* - one's own)
Extraterritoriality (Latin: *extra* + *terra, terrae* - earth, land)
Factum (Latin: *factum, facti* - fact, deed)

LIST OF TERMS

Federalism (Latin: *foedus, foederis* - treaty, league, alliance)
Fiduciary (Latin: *fidus* - faithful)
Fieri facias (Latin: *fieri* - to become + *facere* - to cause, do, make)
Fructus naturales/ industriales (Latin: *fructus, fructus* - fruit)
Functus officio (Latin: *fungi* - to perform, execute + *officium, officii* - office, duty)
Governance (Latin: *gubernare* - to direct, rule)
Grievance (Latin: *gravis* - heavy, painful)
Habeas corpus (Latin: *habere* - to have + *corpus, corporis* - body)
Hostis humani generis (Latin: *hostis, hostis* - enemy + *humanus* - human + *genus, generis* - kind, origin)
Hypotheca (Latin: *hypotheca, hypothecae* - pledge, security)
Ignorantia juris non excusat (Latin: *ignorantia, ignorantiae* - ignorance + *ius, iuris* - law, right + *non* + *excusare* - to excuse, justify)
In absentia (Latin: *in* + *absentia, absentiae* - absence)
In camera (Latin: *in* + *camera, camerae* - room, chamber)
In dubio pro reo (Latin: *in* + *dubium, dubii* - doubt + *pro* + *reus, rei* - defendant, accused, culprit)
In flagrante delicto (Latin: *in* + *flagrare* - to be on fire + *delictum, delicti* - crime, offense)
In limine (Latin: *in* + *limen, liminis* - threshold, entrance)
In loco parentis (Latin: *in* + *locus, loci* - place + *parens, parentis* - parent)
In pari delicto (Latin: *in* + *par, paris* - equal + *delictum, delicti* - fault, offense)
In re (Latin: *in* + *res, rei* - thing, matter)
In rem (Latin: *in* - against + *res, rei* - thing)
Injunction (Latin: *iniungere* - to join together)
Innuendo (Latin: *in* + *nuere* - to nod)
Inter alia (Latin: *inter* + *alius* - other)
Inter partes (Latin: *inter* + *pars, partis* - part, party)
Inter vivos (Latin: *inter* + *vivus* - living)

LIST OF TERMS

Interpretive (Latin: *inter*)
Intervention (Latin: *inter* + *venire* - to come)
Ipso facto (Latin: *ipse* - itself + *factum, facti* - fact, deed)
Ipso jure (Latin: *ipse* - itself + *ius, iuris* - law, right)
Iura novit curia (Latin: *ius, iuris* - law, right + *noscere* - to know + *curia, curiae* - senate, court)
Ius ad bellum (Latin: *ius, iuris* - law, right + *ad* + *bellum, belli* - war)
Ius cogens (Latin: *ius, iuris* - law, right + *cogere* - to gather, compel)
Ius gentium (Latin: *ius, iuris* - law, right + *gens, gentis* - tribe, nation)
Ius in bello (Latin: *ius, iuris* - law, right + *in* + *bellum, belli* - war)
Joinder (Latin: *iungere* - to join together, unite)
Jurisdiction (Latin: *ius, iuris* - law, right + *dicere* - to speak)
Jurisprudence (Latin: *ius, iuris* - law, justice + *prudentia, prudentiae* - wisdom)
Lease (Latin: *laxare* - to loosen)
Lex situs (Latin: *lex, legis* - law + *situs, situs* - situation, position)
Lex talionis (Latin: *lex, legis* - law + *talio, talionis* - retaliation)
Liability (Latin: *ligare* - to bind, tie)
Libel (Latin: *libellus, libelli* - little book)
Licensing (Latin: *licere* - to be allowed, be lawful)
Lis pendens (Latin: *lis, litis* - suit/lawsuit + *pendere* - to hang)
Litigation (Latin: *lis, litis* - lawsuit, quarrel + *agere* - to drive forward)
Locus standi (Latin: *locus, loci* - place + *stare* - to stand)
Mandamus (Latin: *mandare* - to command)
Mare liberum (Latin: *mare, maris* - sea + *liber* - free)
Mens Rea (Latin: *mens, mentis* - mind + *rea* - guilty)
Merger (Latin: *mergere* - to dip in, plunge, overwhelm)
Mortgage (Latin: *mors, mortis* - death)
Multilateral (Latin: *multus* - many + *latus, lateris* - the side)
Mutatis mutandis (Latin: *mutare* - to change)
Nationality (Latin: *natio, nationis* - birth, origin)

LIST OF TERMS

Ne exeat (Latin: *ne* + *exire* - to go)
Negligence (Latin: *ne* + *legere* - to choose, select)
Nemo dat quod non habet (Latin: *nemo, neminis* - no one + *dare* - to give + *quis* - who, which + *non* + *habere* - to have)
Nemo judex in causa sua (Latin: *nemo, neminis* - no one + *iudex, iudicis* - judge + *in* + *causa, causae* - reason, case + *suus* - one's own)
Neutrality (Latin: *neuter* - neither)
Nolle prosequi (Latin: *nolle* - to be unwilling + *prosequi* - to pursue)
Nolo contendere (Latin: *nolle* - to be unwilling + *contendere* - to stretch)
Non bis in idem (Latin: *non* + *bis* - twice + *in* + *idem* - the same)
Non compos mentis (Latin: *non* + *compos, compotis* - mastery + *mens, mentis* - mind)
Non est factum (Latin: *non* + *factum, facti* - fact, deed)
Non sequitur (Latin: *non* + *sequi* - to follow)
Noncompete (Latin: *non* + *cum* + *petere* - to strive, seek)
Notary (Latin: *nota, notae* - letter, note)
Novus actus interveniens (Latin: *novus* - new + *actus, actus* - act, deed + *intervenire* - to come between)
Nuisance (Latin: *nocere* - to hurt, harm)
Nullum crimen sine lege (Latin: *nullus, nulli* - no one + *crimen, criminis* - punishment, indictment + *sine* + *lex, legis* - law)
Nunc pro tunc (Latin: *nunc* - now + *pro* + *tunc* - then)
Nuptial (Latin: *nubere* - to marry)
Obiter dictum (Latin: *obiter* - in passing + *dicere* - to say)
Objection (Latin: *ob* - in front of, against + *iacere* - to throw)
Occupation (Latin: *ob* + *capere* - to take, capture)
Onus probandi (Latin: *onus, oneris* - burden, cargo + *probare* - to try, test)
Option (Latin: *optare* - to choose, wish)
Pacta sunt servanda (Latin: *pactum, pacti* - agreement + *servare* - to save)
Parens patriae (Latin: *parens, parentis* - parent + *patria, patriae* - fatherland, country)

LIST OF TERMS

Partnership (Latin: *pars, partis* - part, piece)
Passport (Latin: *passus, passus* - step, pace + *portus, portus* - harbor)
Paternity (Latin: *pater, patris* - father)
Pendete lite (Latin: *pendere* - to hang + *lis, litis* - lawsuit)
Per curiam (Latin: *per* + *curia, curiae* - court, senate)
Per diem (Latin: *per* + *dies, diei* - day)
Per se (Latin: *per* + *se* - itself)
Per stirpes (Latin: *per* + *stirps, stirpis* - stock, plant)
Persona non grata (Latin: *persona, personae* - person + *non* + *gratia, gratiae* - goodwill, favor, esteem)
Post hoc ergo propter hoc (Latin: *post* + *hic* - this + *ergo* - therefore + *propter* - on account of + *hic* - this)
Post mortem (Latin: *post* + *mors, mortis* - death)
Preamble (Latin: *pre* + *ambulare*) - to walk
Precedent (Latin: *prae* + *cedere* - to go, march)
Preemption (Latin: *pre* + *emere* - to buy)
Prima facie (Latin: *primus* - first + *facies, faciei* - face, appearance)
Privacy (Latin: *privus* - one's own, individual)
Privilege (Latin: *privus* - one's own, individual + *lex, legis* - law)
Pro bono (publico) (Latin: *pro* + *bonus, boni* - good + *publicus* - public)
Pro forma (Latin: *pro* + *forma, formae* - form, shape)
Pro rata (Latin: *pro* + *reri* - to think)
Pro se (Latin: *pro* + *se* - oneself)
Pro tempore (Latin: *pro* + *tempus, temporis* - time)
Probate (Latin: *probare* - to try, test, prove)
Promulgation (Latin: *pro* + *mulgere* - to milk)
Prospectus (Latin: *pro* - forward + *specere* - to look at)
Provision (Latin: *pro* + *videre* - to see)
Proxy (Latin: *pro* + *curare* - to care for)
Quantum (meruit) (Latin: *quantum* - how much + *merere* - to earn, deserve)

LIST OF TERMS

Quasi (Latin: *quasi* - as if)
Quid pro quo (Latin: *quis* - who, which, something + *pro*)
Quod erat demonstrandum (Q.E.D.) (Latin: *qui* - which + *demonstrare* - to show)
Quorum (Latin: *qui* - who)
Ratio decidendi (Latin: *ratio, rationis* - reason + *decidere* - to decide)
Rebus sic stantibus (Latin: *res, rei* - thing + *sic* - thus + *stare* - to stand)
Recognition (Latin: *re* + *cognoscere* - to learn, become acquainted with)
Reductio ad absurdum (Latin: *re* + *ductio, ductionis* - leading away + *ad* + *absurdus* - absurd, nonsensical)
Refugee (Latin: *re* + *fugere* - to flee)
Refund (Latin: *re* + *fundere* - to pour)
Regulation (Latin: *regulare* - to control by rule)
Repudiation (Latin: *repudium, repudii* - divorce, rejection)
Res derelictae (Latin: *res, rei* - thing + *derelinquere* - to leave behind)
Res gestae (Latin: *res, rei* - thing + *gerere* - to bear, wage)
Res ipsa loquitur (Latin: *res, rei* - thing + *ipse* - itself + *loqui* - to speak)
Res judicata (Latin: *res, rei* - thing + *iudicare* - to judge)
Residence (Latin: *re* + *sedere* - to sit)
Respondeat superior (Latin: *re* + *spondere* - to answer + superior - higher)
Respondent (Latin: *re* + *spondere* - to pledge)
Restitutio ad integrum (Latin: *restitutio, restitutionis* - reinstatement + *ad* + *integer* - untouched, whole)
Restructuring (Latin: *re* + *struere* - to build)
Retaliation (Latin: *retaliare* - to pay back in kind)
Riparian (Latin: *ripa, ripae* - bank, shore)
Rulemaking (Latin: *regula, regulae* - rule, straight piece of wood)
Safety (Latin: *salus, salutis* - health, prosperity)
Sanction (Latin: *sancire* - to decree, devote)
Scienter (Latin: *scienter* - skillfully, consciously)
Seniority (Latin: *senior* - older)

LIST OF TERMS

Severance (Latin: *se* + *parare* - to prepare)
Sine qua non (Latin: *sine* + *quis* - who, which, something + *non*)
Situs (Latin: *situs, situs* - situation, position)
Sovereignty (Latin: *super*)
Speculation (Latin: *specere* - to look, view)
Stare decisis (Latin: *stare* - to stand + *decidere* - to decide)
Status quo (Latin: *status, status* - position, state + *qui* - who, which)
Stet (Latin: *stare* - to stand)
Strict (Latin: *stringere* - to draw tight)
Stricto sensu (Latin: *strictus* - tight, close + *sensus, sensus* - sense)
Sua sponte (Latin: *suus* - its own + *spons, spontis* - free will)
Sub judice (Latin: *sub* + *iudex, iudicis* - judge)
Sub silentio (Latin: *sub* + *silentium, silentii* - silence)
Subpoena (Latin: *sub* + *poena* - punishment, penalty)
Subsidiary (Latin: *sub* + *sedere* - to sit)
Sui generis (Latin: *suus* - its own + *genus, generis* - kind, origin)
Supremacy (Latin: *supremus* - highest)
Surrogacy (Latin: *sub* + *rogare* - to ask, propose)
Sustained (Latin: *sub* + *tenere* - to hold)
Tenure (Latin: *tenere* - to hold)
Termination (Latin: *terminus, termini* - boundary, end)
Terra nullius (Latin: *terra, terrae* - earth, land + *nullus, nulli* - no one)
Ubi jus ibi remedium (Latin: *ubi* - where + *ius, iuris* - law, right + *ibi* - there + *remedium, remedii* - remedy, cure)
Ultra vires (Latin: *ultra* - beyond + *vis, viris* - strength, power)
Union (Latin: *unus* - one)
Uti possidetis, ita possideatis (Latin: *uti* - as + *possidere* - to hold + *ita* - thus, so)
Validation (Latin: *valere* - to be well, strong)
Verdict (Latin: *verus* - true + *dicere* - to speak)

LIST OF TERMS

Veto (Latin: vetare - to forbid, prohibit)
Vicarious (Latin: vicis, vicis - change, succession, exchange)
Vigilantibus non dormientibus iura subveniunt (Latin: vigilans, vigilantis - vigilant, alert + non + dormire - to sleep + ius, iuris - law, right + subvenire - to assist)
Visitation (Latin: videre - to see)

About Us

Eshaan Vasudev

Eshaan Vasudev is a high school student at the University School of Milwaukee. He was introduced to Latin and the classics in his freshman year of high school, and since then has been very passionate about studying the ancient world, working to promote it as President of the Wisconsin Junior Classical League. He hopes to major in Classics in his undergraduate studies and pursue a pre-medical track.

Claire Tian

Claire is a high school student at Brookfield Academy and seven-year Latin scholar. As a nationally recognized member of the JCL and editor intern with Dickinson College Commentaries, she applies her classical learnings to modern disciplines. As President of both her school's Latin Club and Student Council and co-captain of her school's Mock Trial team, she leads initiatives to spread the significance of classical knowledge today.

Aida El-Hajjar

Aida El-Hajjar is a high school student at the University School of Milwaukee, with a passion for classics, science, and art. She began creating art during the pandemic and now enjoys combining it with her other interests. Aida plans to pursue a career as a psychiatrist as well as continuing to pursue the arts in the future.

Mia Lucke

Mia Lucke is a student at the University School of Milwaukee, with a passion for art, psychology, literature and writing. She often performs poetry at open mics or fundraising events, exploring her own retellings of the world in her work. She plans to become an author and illustrator, and continue to pursue her love of the classics.

Ronald D. Roessler, MD

Ron Roessler majored in Classics at Princeton University and works as both an Emergency Room physician and a Latin teacher. In addition to more than four decades of experience studying, teaching, and coaching Latin, Dr. Roessler has been inducted into the National Junior Classical League Hall of Fame as both a player and a coach.

Andrew Mills

Andrew Mills is the Latin teacher at the University School of Milwaukee. He's been teaching for around 20 years and has taught Latin, History, and English at several schools all over the U.S. and Canada at many levels. He has a strong passion for Latin, Experimental Archaeology, Ancient Religion and Philosophy, Ancient Magic, Mythology, the Roman Army, and supporting all of his students in finding their own sense of joy in the study of Classics.

Fifty percent of the proceeds from the sale of this book will be donated to Wisconsin Junior Classical League (WJCL), National Junior Classical League (NJCL) and to promote Latin education.

www.ingramcontent.com/pod-product-compliance
Lightning Source LLC
LaVergne TN
LVHW010835120826
845149LV00017B/1471

* 9 7 9 8 9 9 9 3 3 8 8 4 6 *